The Biblical Qualifications of Church Leaders

*The 26 Mandatory Biblical Requirements
for Church Pastors, Elders, and Bishops
Based on 1 Timothy 3 and Titus 1*

Charlie Avila

The material in this book was first taught to local church leaders in Fresno and presented on the teacherofthebible.com website in the United States.

Clovis Christian Center
3606 N. Fowler Ave
Fresno, California, USA 93727-1124

ISBN: **9798614088668**
(Softcover Edition)

Printed in the United States

CONTENTS

DEDICATION

This book is affectionately dedicated to Pastor Thomas Kirk Hanger – a humble leader, a Christ-like example, a missionary statesman, and faithful and dedicated servant of the Lord. He has shown me and so many other leaders, pastors, and Christians tremendous grace, encouragement, and support. Thank you for all that you do for Christ and His church. No words could properly express my appreciation.

PREFACE

The twenty-six biblical qualifications for church elders/bishops found in 1 Timothy 3 and Titus 1 are a supernatural revelation given to the apostle Paul by the Holy Spirit. It is such a revealing study into God's holiness and standards. The Lord really loves His church, and He requires that only well-qualified believers be appointed and placed in leadership positions.

It is a serious error to put people in as elders, pastors, and bishops who are not qualified. Regularly, I see local churches put people in who should never be a church leader. It opens the door to accusations and the devil's traps. Twice, Paul said that if you put unqualified people in as elders, the devil will get into your church (1 Timothy 3:6-7).

Having said that, this book was not written to create impossible standards that no one can meet. Paul said that elders and bishops (overseers) must be *blameless*, not *sinless*. If the requirement was "sinless," then none of us would qualify. Only the Lord Jesus Christ is sinless.

One of the main motivations I had for writing this book was to show the three main areas of evaluation of a potential elder's life. The criterion for selected leaders is absolutely critical to the life and well-being of any church or ministry. Nineteen of the qualifications involve the person's CHARACTER; five deal with his FAMILY (wife and children); and only two with his MINISTRY (abilities). I can't emphasize how important this is. Many times, pastors and churches appoint people based on ministry ability and gifting only, but if a potential candidate has certain character flaws and problems with his wife and children, it doesn't really matter how well he can teach. As one commentator writes, "No intellectual power or pulpit brilliancy can atone for the lack of solid Christian virtues and a blameless life."

A word about nomenclature. More than 95% of today's church leaders (elders/pastors/teachers) are men. Rather than write he/she or "he or she" throughout the book, I've written it from a male perspective. Both 1 Timothy 3 and Titus 1 assume that the local church leaders are men because Paul writes about the elder's "wife" and "*his* children." He'll also use the pronoun, "he," seven times when describing qualifications.

I titled this book, *"The Biblical Qualifications of CHURCH LEADERS."* There are so many titles that different churches, denominations, fellowships, and ministry associations use for their ministers. A bishop in one group is a pastor in another; an elder in one church is an overseer in another. All the chapter titles begin with "The Church Leader..." and then lists the qualification. So, whenever I write about a "church leader" in this book, I'm referring to the "elders" and "bishops" of 1 Timothy 3 and Titus 1. The preferred title in the book of Acts and the epistles is "elder," so most of my writing uses that name. Interestingly, the main leader at most of our local churches is known as "pastor;" and yet, "pastor" is never mentioned in the Pastoral Epistles (1 Timothy, 2 Timothy, Titus). But, "elders," "bishops," and even "deacons" are mentioned eleven times by name.

Many churches appoint people as "deacons" and they are really the "elders." However, a deacon (diakonos) is a servant (*"serve* as deacons" and "those who have *served* well as deacons" – 1 Timothy 3:10, 13). A "diakonos" was someone "who ran errands." On the other hand, an elder/bishop is one who teaches Scripture. This book is not about deacons, but about elders.

Many years ago, a member of our church asked me if there was a test he could take that would help him evaluate where he was as a Christian believer. "Is there a standard I can measure myself against that would let me know how well I'm living my life in Christ?" I told him, "Brother, look carefully at all the qualifications for church elders found in 1 Timothy 3 and Titus 1. These are godly standards. All Christians should aspire to live like these elders." Paul wrote in 2 Corinthians 13:5, "Examine yourselves to see whether you are in the faith; test yourselves. Do you not realize that Christ Jesus is in you – unless, of course, you fail the test?" How does your Christian life look compared to the twenty-six qualifications found in this book?

The book includes study questions and a bibliography in the back for further study in small groups or individually.

May the Lord give you insight, revelation, and wisdom as you study this book. May all the churches and ministries in the body of Christ have qualified people in positions of leadership.

Jesus Christ is Lord. To God be the glory.

Charlie Avila, March 2023

The 26 Biblical Qualifications for Church Leaders

1 The Church Leader Must Be Blameless
2 The Church Leader Must Have a Good Reputation
3 The Church Leader Must Be of Good Behavior
4 The Church Leader Must Be a Lover of Good Things

5 The Church Leader Must Be Hospitable
6 The Church Leader Must Be Temperate
7 The Church Leader Must Be Sober-Minded
8 The Church Leader Must Be Self-Controlled

9 The Church Leader Must Be Just
10 The Church Leader Must Be Holy
11 The Church Leader Must Be Gentle
12 The Church Leader Must Not Be Quarrelsome

13 The Church Leader Must Not Be Violent
14 The Church Leader Must Not Be Soon Angry
15 The Church Leader Must Not Be Self-Willed
16 The Church Leader Must Not Be Greedy for Money

17 The Church Leader Must Not Be Covetous
18 The Church Leader Must Not Be Given to Wine
19 The Church Leader Must Not Be a Novice
20 The Church Leader Must Be the Husband of One Wife

21 The Church Leader Must Rule His Household Well
22 The Church Leader Must Have Believing Children
23 The Church Leader Must Have Children Who are Obedient and Respectful
24 The Church Leader Must Not Have Children Known to Be Wild and Disobedient

25 The Church Leader Must Be Able to Teach
26 The Church Leader Must Encourage and Refute with Sound Doctrine

1

The Church Leader Must Be Blameless

*"A bishop then **must be blameless**."*
(1 Timothy 3:2)

"Appoint elders in every city as I commanded you –
*if a man is **blameless**...for a bishop must be*
***blameless**."*
(Titus 1:5-7)

The very first requirement for a church elder or bishop is that he must be "blameless" or "above reproach." *This is always first.* This is emphasized so strongly by Paul that the Holy Spirit moved on him to write it three times, and each time it was listed first before any other qualification. Guthrie says it stands first because it is "indispensable to the Christian minister's character"[1] and Mounce calls it "the summary title and Paul's primary concern."[2]

Right after writing, "This is a faithful saying: If a man desires the position of a bishop, he desires a good work," he then

---

[1] *The Pastoral Epistles*, Donald Guthrie, Tyndale New Testament Commentaries, Revised Edition, Eerdmans Publishing, Grand Rapids, Michigan, page 92.
[2] *Pastoral Epistles*, William D. Mounce, Word Biblical Commentary, Volume 46, Zondervan, Grand Rapids, Michigan, page 388.

1

writes, "A bishop must be *blameless*." Right after writing, "Set in order the things that are lacking, and appoint elders in every city as I commanded you," he then writes, only "if a man is *blameless*." Then he repeats it again in the next verse, "For a bishop must be *blameless*."[3] *The only qualification that qualifies all the others is that a church leader must be blameless.* Kelly rightly calls it the "all-embracing requirement"[4] and one early church father wrote, "All possible qualifications are included in one."[5] He must be blameless because he is being entrusted with God's work.

This is mandatory. *He MUST BE* blameless.[6] This is tremendously important. In fact, this also becomes the main requirement to qualify deacons: "But let these also first be tested; then let them serve as deacons, being found *blameless*."[7]

I like the strong wording of one author: "An elder represents God. He is entrusted with God's household, God's possessions, God's treasures, and God's riches. He acts on behalf of God's interests. An elder is accountable and responsible to God. A noble occupation thus demands a noble character."[8]

First of all, notice immediately that he didn't say "sinless," but "blameless." If he wrote "sinless," no one would qualify except Jesus. No, he wrote "blameless." Stott writes, "This cannot mean 'faultless,' or no child of Adam would ever

---

[3] See 1 Timothy 3:1-2, Titus 1:6, and Titus 1:7.

[4] *A Commentary on the Pastoral Epistles*, J. N. D. Kelly, Baker Book House, Grand Rapids, Michigan, page 75. Knight calls it "the overall requirement," see page 289 of his *The Pastoral Epistles* (NIGTC).

[5] *Ancient Christian Commentary on Scripture*, Volume IX, 1 Timothy, Edited by Peter Gorday, Inter-Varsity Press, Downers Grove, Illinois, page 170. See the commentary of Gregory of Nyssa.

[6] See Robert W. Yarbrough's outstanding breakdown of the Greek word, "dei," in his commentary, *The Letters of Timothy and Titus*, pages 193-194. He translates "dei" as "it is necessary" and says "it conveys moral and often divinely demanded necessity." "Dei" is found eight times in the Pastoral Epistles.

[7] See 1 Timothy 3:10.

[8] *Biblical Eldership*, Alexander Strauch, An Urgent Call to Restore Biblical Church Leadership, Lewis and Roth Publishers, Littleton, Colorado, page 172.

qualify for a share in the oversight."[9] One translation uses "of blameless reputation," "of unquestioned integrity," and "of unimpeachable virtue"[10] for the three appearances of "blameless."

It's important to define this word from the original languages because we will see right away what "blameless" means.

Paul used two different Greek words with the same basic meaning. In 1 Timothy 3:2, the Greek word means, "not arrested" or "to not seize or to lay hold of you." It was a legal term that means no one can bring a charge against you. One translation renders the verse, "An elder must not give people a reason to criticize him," and another says, "An elder must be such a good man that no one can rightly criticize him."

In Titus 1:6 and 1:7, he uses a word that means "to not call in a debt or demand; to bring no charge or accusation." Simply put, no one can even bring an accusation against you for any inappropriate behavior. Interestingly, it is used in Acts 19:40 when a riot nearly broke out in Ephesus: "For we are in danger of *being called into question* for today's uproar, there being no reason which we may give to account for this disorderly gathering." The people were being "disorderly" which caused an "uproar," so they were in danger of "being called into question."[11] Paul uses this Greek root word for "blameless" in his instruction to Titus. In other words, don't put in elders or pastors who are "disorderly" and can "be called into question." John Calvin defines it as someone who "should not be tainted with any disgrace that might detract from his authority."[12]

The Hebrew word is very similar. When the Lord appeared to Abram in Genesis 17:1, He said, "I am Almighty God; walk before Me and be blameless." The word here means "to be entire or whole (morally); to be full of integrity and truth." It is translated more than fifty times as "without blemish" or "without

---

[9] *The Message of 1 Timothy & Titus*, John R. W. Stott, The Bible Speaks Today, Inter-Varsity Press, Downers Grove, Illinois, page 92.

[10] See the J. B. Phillips Translation of 1 Timothy 3:2 and Titus 1:6-7.

[11] Colossians 1:22 (NIV) translates the same Greek word as "free from accusation."

[12] *1 & 2 Timothy & Titus*, John Calvin, The Crossway Classic Commentaries, Crossway Books, Wheaton, Illinois, page 53.

spot" (speaking of sacrificial animals offered to the Lord), and nine times as "upright" or "undefiled" in the Psalms and Proverbs.

Many years ago, a man and his wife came to our church. He was an associate pastor at another church for a few years, and he ran a men's Christian rehabilitation home in a city north of us. He really liked our church and wanted to get involved as soon as possible. He contacted me to find out when and where he could begin to minister.

I interviewed both the man and his wife in one of our Sunday School classrooms. Somehow in our conversation, the wife mentioned that her husband had a suspended driver's license. As I probed further, she told me that he had six outstanding tickets, including two for speeding. He was driving daily on a suspended license.

I asked him, "Brother, why do you drive to church services every week on a suspended license? Legally, you are not allowed to drive at this time until you take care of these tickets."

I added, "This shows me a lack of integrity because you should not be driving your car. If a police officer pulls you over, you're going to jail. This is clearly wrong."

These statements clearly agitated this man.

I asked him, "How come you haven't taken care of these tickets?"

He said it would cost perhaps thousands of dollars in fees, fines, and legal help to take care of all the tickets. He could not afford to pay all these costs.

His wife had been upset with him for many years because she felt he was skirting the law and not taking care of these violations. She then mentioned that her husband was quite unstable.

I asked, "How so?"

She said that they had moved about sixteen times over the last ten years. She added that he couldn't hold down a job for very long and he was a chain smoker.

Wow, the list was getting longer by the minute! It appeared to me like the wife was airing a lot of frustrations in my presence with the hope that maybe I could encourage him to take care of these charges.

They both began to argue in my presence, and I had to stop them. I simply told the man that he needed to take care of these tickets and some other things before I could consider him for any type of eldership position in the church. With that comment, a big frown came across his face.

The clincher for him was when I said, "Brother, what would happen if one of these police officers who gave you a ticket came to one of the services? Or what if a government official who knew your driving history came to hear you preach? Do you think they would be open to hear you teach when you have six outstanding tickets that you've never taken care of?"

I finished with these words: "Bob, 1 Timothy 3:7 says of church leaders, 'He must also have a good reputation with outsiders, so that he will not fall into disgrace and into the devil's trap.' One translation says, 'People outside the church must speak well of him.' Our lives as elders must be so spotless that we're not even supposed to 'listen to an accusation against an elder unless it is confirmed by two or three witnesses. Those who sin should be reprimanded in front of the whole church; this will serve as a strong warning to others.'"[13]

"Friend, you're not qualified to lead."

With that final comment, he gathered his items and walked out of the door. I never saw him again.

I ask all church leaders, how can we stand behind the pulpit and tell other believers how to live the Christian life, when our own life is completely out of order? We have too much blame. We don't have a good reputation. People will not believe us. They won't trust us and the Word of God will fall into disrepute. No, we can't allow that to happen. The elder must be blameless!

Upon careful examination, the word "blameless" is found throughout the Bible. The Lord commanded the Israelites, "You shall be *blameless* before the Lord your God." Twice, the Lord told Satan of Job, "Have you considered My servant Job, that there is none like him on the earth, a *blameless* and upright man, one who fears God and shuns evil?" The psalmist prayed, "Keep your servant also from willful sins; may they not rule over me. Then will I be *blameless*, innocent of great transgression." David wrote,

---

[13] See 1 Timothy 5:19-20.

"Mark the *blameless* man, and observe the upright; for the future of that man is peace." The wisdom of God says, "For the upright will dwell in the land, and the *blameless* will remain in it" and "righteousness guards him whose way is *blameless*." Zachariah and Elizabeth "were both righteous before God, walking in all the commandments and ordinances of the Lord *blameless*."[14] Yes, the Bible says a lot about being blameless!

Although the word "blameless" appears in many places of the Bible, it is not very obvious. It is a very subtle word. We read over it without paying much attention. It seems to be hiding in the background. Honestly, when was the last time you heard a sermon on being blameless?

At the end of this chapter, I will give some practical instruction on living a blameless life as a pastor or church leader, but I want to first summarize, with some brief comments, how this word is used in the New Testament, especially by the apostle Paul. To be blameless is very important to the heart of Father God. This is the one biblical requirement for church leaders listed before all others and it is mentioned more than any others. Christians must stop and take notice. This really is a big deal. You cannot gloss over this truth when you're considering people for ministry leadership. I've seen disastrous results in many churches when they ignore this requirement.

Notice how Paul used this word:

1 Corinthians 1:8 – "*He will keep you strong to the end, so that you will be blameless on the day of our Lord Jesus Christ.*" Some other translations render this Greek word for "blameless" as "completely innocent," "free from all blame," or "there will be no wrong in you." God wants us blameless all the way until Jesus returns on the Day of the Lord (when Jesus judges everyone). The Lord desires you to be without any blame on Judgment Day. Like Jude 24, "Now to Him who is able to keep you from falling, and to present you *faultless* before the presence of His glory with exceeding joy." One translation says "without a single fault." Faultless and blameless have the same meaning. God is able to do this in your life.

---

[14] See Deuteronomy 18:13; Job 1:8, 2:3; Psalm 19:13, 37:37; Proverbs 2:21, 13:6; Luke 1:6.

Philippians 2:14-15 – *"Do everything without complaining or arguing, that you may become blameless and harmless, children of God without fault in the midst of a crooked and perverse generation, among whom you shine as lights in the world."* This is a very powerful verse. Most Christians do the opposite – they do everything with complaining and arguing!

Paul says this is how you're going to be "blameless," "harmless," and "without fault" in this crooked and perverse generation. This is how we're going to shine as lights in the world. This is how you "work out your salvation with fear and trembling" (v12). This is how you "work out" what God is "working in."

Colossians 1:21-22 – *"...yet now He has reconciled in the body of His flesh through death, to present you holy, and blameless, and above reproach in His sight."* The NIV uses "without blemish." No one can be blameless in God's sight apart from the sacrifice of Jesus Christ on Calvary's cross. He reconciled us through His death to present us blameless before God.

Interestingly, the apostle Peter would use this same Greek word in 1 Peter 1:19 to describe "the precious blood of Christ," as of "a lamb *without blemish* and without spot." Paul used the word in Ephesians 1:4, when he wrote, "God chose us in Him before the foundation of the world, that we should be holy and *without blame* before Him in love."

1 Thessalonians 3:13 – *"So that He may establish your hearts blameless in holiness before our God and Father at the coming of our Lord Jesus Christ with all His saints."* Years ago, I did a verse-by-verse class on 1 Thessalonians. The theme of this book is the 2nd Coming of Jesus. However, the one statement from this book that stood out for me is that magnificent phrase – "Blameless in holiness." What a beautiful statement! Christians have "no blame" regarding holiness. We are commanded to live holy lives. That is, we are to have lives without blame. Again, God wants to establish this in our hearts "at the coming of the Lord Jesus Christ." When Jesus comes, we want to be "blameless in holiness!"

1 Thessalonians 5:23 – *"Now may the God of peace Himself sanctify you completely; and may your whole spirit, soul, and body be preserved blameless at the coming of our Lord Jesus*

Christ." This may be my favorite verse on the blameless life. Do we hear the powerful wording here? This is so comprehensive and total. Notice the words – "completely," "through and through" (NIV), "in every way" (NLT); "your whole spirit, soul, and body." It's as if God demands every fiber of our being to be holy and blameless. And He again wants this to be our standing before Him "at the coming of our Lord Jesus Christ." When He comes, many will not be ready.

Paul had already used this word in addressing the Thessalonians in the 2nd Chapter. He writes, "You are witnesses, and God also, how devoutly and justly and *blamelessly* we behaved ourselves among you who believe" (2:10). The behavior of Paul and the other apostles was "blameless." More than that, they were "devout" and "just." There was nothing anyone could say against them.

1 Timothy 5:7 – "*And these things command, that they may be blameless.*" When Paul said a few verses earlier – "That a bishop then must be *blameless*" – he used the same Greek word as you find here in 5:7. He'll use it again in 1 Timothy 6:14.[15]

Paul was teaching Timothy how to treat "older men and older women," "younger men and younger women," and "widows." He had to teach "children and grandchildren" how to treat their mothers and grandmothers. Timothy had to command them to take care of things "at home" (v4) so they would properly take care of things "within their household." To not do so was to act "worse than an unbeliever" (v8). Being blameless was God's requirement for all Christians, and it all started at home.

Let's look at the last verse: 1 Timothy 6:14 – "*That you keep this commandment without spot, blameless until our Lord Jesus Christ's appearing.*" Paul, using one Greek imperative verb after another, commands Timothy to "flee," "pursue," "fight," and "lay hold" (verses 11-12). These are God's "commandments." There's that phrase again that is often associated with "blameless" – "without spot."[16] And again, he had to keep this "blameless until

---

[15] In fact, these are the only three places in the entire New Testament where this Greek word is used – 1 Timothy 3:2, 5:7, and 6:14.

[16] Recall Paul's well-known words in Ephesians 5:27, "That He might present her to Himself a glorious church, not having spot or wrinkle or any such thing, but that she should be holy and without blemish."

our Lord Jesus Christ's appearing." You must be blameless when Jesus comes.

With those New Testament verses as a background, let me share with you four practical areas where pastors/elders must live a blameless life.

Your Finances. I'm not sure why this is the case, but so many ministers of the gospel have their personal, church, or ministry finances out of order. They owe people money. The church is in debt. The bookkeeping is disorganized. This is a very bad testimony.

If you are a pastor, you need to pay your bills on time – *all the time!* Never owe anyone anything. If you're taking advantage of the church's finances, stop it. Do everything financially with complete integrity. I know several churches and pastors who have not reconciled any bank statements for the church in years. This is a bad witness. I know a well-known traveling evangelist who would not preach in churches unless they gave him a minimum of $2,500-$3,000 for a Sunday service. I know a church that never pulled permits with the city to do any of their building projects. This was a disaster. I know a pastor who gave church money to one of his in-laws so he could catch up on his bills. This is illegal. When it comes to handling church money, pastors must be "without blemish" and "without spot."

Your Weight. I know this is going to get me into a lot of trouble. Paul wrote, "But I discipline my body and bring it into subjection, lest, when I have preached to others, I myself should become disqualified." Another translation reads, "I keep my body under control and make it my slave, so I won't lose out after telling the good news to others."[17] So many pastors and church leaders have out of control appetites. Many are in very poor physical health, and not because of age. They tell others about living a disciplined life, and they have no discipline themselves. A disciple is a disciplined person, and we must discipline our body or we're disqualified. How will you teach others about "prayer and fasting" when it's obvious you never do? No sumo wrestler ever entered a marathon race! How can you run the race with

---

[17] See 1 Corinthians 9:27.

endurance when you're completely out of shape? Don't you realize that your physical body is the temple of the Holy Spirit?

Go get a physical. Lose weight. Control your appetite. Exercise. Don't let your overweight body disqualify you from the prize or from preaching and leading a church.

Your Marriage. No pastor will last long in the ministry without a strong marriage. Many ministers tell others to put their "family above the ministry," but they themselves rarely do. I just heard a few weeks ago of another pastor whose marriage has failed and his wife left him. He's still running the church. I just need to quote Paul's convicting question for elders and bishops in 1 Timothy 3:5 – "If a man does not know how to rule his own house, how will he take care of the church of God?"

As a church leader, you need to spend a lot of quiet, unrushed time with your wife. There's one thing I've learned from my years in the ministry – the people of God will definitely see all the cracks in your marriage. They are impossible to hide when you're under the tremendous strain of ministry pressure. Too many gifted church leaders have had affairs, divorces, and emotional breakdowns because of weak marriages. *Your ministry will only be as strong as your marriage.* If you are not close to your wife, the devil will send pretty little girls your way. They will sweet talk you right into the bedroom.

Your Appearance. After studying Romans 14 very carefully over the years, I've come to this conclusion: When it comes to issues of conscience, I do everything unto Jesus and for the glory of God. I love that word in Colossians 3:17, "Whatever you do in word or deed, do all in the name of the Lord Jesus." Paul also said, "Whether you eat or drink, or whatever you do, do all to the glory of God." I like something else he said to the Corinthians – "We give no offense in anything that our ministry may not be blamed."[18] Don't do anything that will cause your ministry to be blamed. Be blameless.

When I dress myself for a church service, I don't "dress to impress." I dress to present myself to Jesus Christ. I want to be presentable to Him before anyone else. I never want to cause another brother to stumble.

---

[18] See 1 Corinthians 10:31 and 2 Corinthians 6:3.

There used to be a time when nearly all ministers of the gospel wore a suit and tie. This was normal. This was the standard. There was always a professional bearing among the clergy. *Today, people call it legalism.* Today, they say we're out of touch. Today, they say we're not hip or cool. What is in today are torn jeans, shoes with no socks, muscle shirts, long hair, gold chains and expensive jewelry. Ministers look like people in the world or those on the street.

I saw a minister of a large church recently with jeans that had holes throughout, cuffed up at the bottom to reveal his slip-on shoes with no socks. I was impressed by the hairs on his ankles! He wore an old tee-shirt with an old sweater. To be honest, he looked like a tramp. But this is normal now. It's okay to wear shorts, sweat pants, and clothes that have not been ironed. "We're free." "Jesus doesn't care how we look." "We want to be cool."

In my view, they are actually drawing attention to themselves. It's not about Jesus and His kingdom; it's about looking like everyone else so they'll say we're cool. I remember an evangelist who wore a $5,000 watch that had a band made of shiny 24K gold and the face was studded with many diamonds. It glittered whenever any light hit it. I spent the whole time staring at his watch instead of listening to his sermon. He also told us at the beginning of the message how much he has paid for the watch. It was all very distracting.

I'll never forget a worship leader I saw at a large church in Sacramento. He is a body builder/weight lifter type. He has large biceps with lots of tattoos. He wore a muscle shirt along with pants that were so tight, he must have spray painted them on. He also had large, black combat boots. He looked militant. His shaved head gave him an intimidating appearance. Whenever he would lift his hands during a song, he would invariably flex his biceps. I had to close my eyes during the worship service because I was spending too much time looking at his impressive physique. You had this feeling that he enjoyed everyone staring at him.

Whatever you believe about these things, I strongly believe that your appearance should be clean, decent, respectful, and honorable. I want to point people to Christ, not my clothes! When it comes to your personal appearance, be blameless. Remember: You represent Christ to others.

The elder's ministry is a "*good* work." Therefore, he must have "a *good* testimony," be of "*good* behavior," and be "a lover of what is *good*." In the next three chapters, let's talk about the "good things" of a leader's character.

2

The Church Leader Must Have a Good Reputation

*"Moreover he must **have a good testimony (reputation) among those who are outside**, lest he fall into reproach and the snare of the devil."*
(1 Timothy 3:7)

With most of the qualifications for eldership, Paul will use one or two words, but with this one, he took a whole verse. It is very important.

Did you notice right away in 1 Timothy 3:6 and 3:7 the words, "the devil?" Did you also notice the words, "lest he fall," in both verses? Jesus said, "I saw Satan fall like lightning from heaven."[19] *If you appoint the wrong people into leadership, the devil will get into your church.* If you appoint the wrong people, they will fall just like the devil did. The wrong leaders will bring pride, and wherever pride is, the devil is nearby.

Some translations begin 1 Timothy 3:7 with these words – "He must also have a good reputation with outsiders," "people outside the church must speak well of him," and "an elder must also have the respect of people who are not part of the church." Hiebert calls it "the qualification as to community standing."[20]

---

[19] See Luke 10:18.
[20] *First Timothy*, D. Edmond Hiebert, Everyman's Bible Commentary, Moody Press, page 67.

This brings us back to the first qualification of being "blameless" or "above reproach." "Even unbelievers should have to acknowledge that he is a good person."[21]

Some men told Peter, "Cornelius the centurion, a just man, one who fears God and has a good reputation among all the nation of the Jews."[22] Cornelius would have made a good elder. He had a good reputation with everyone. The apostles told people, "Brethren, seek out from among you seven men of good reputation, full of the Holy Spirit and wisdom, whom we may appoint over this business."[23] Even people who distributed bread to widows had to have "a good reputation."

Guthrie writes, "The non-Christian world has persistently condemned professing Christians whose practice is at variance with their profession. It is not that outsiders are arbiters of the church's choice of its officers, but that no minister will achieve success who has not first gained the confidence of his fellows."[24] Another commentator writes: "The pastor who fails in this respect is liable to incur slander, since unsympathetic outsiders will put the most unfavorable interpretation on his slightest word or deed."[25]

Paul says that the elder must have a "good testimony" with people outside the church. According to several Greek dictionaries, the word for "good," "kalos," means "beautiful; expressing beauty as a harmonious completeness, balance, and proportion." Paul wrote elsewhere that Christians were to "be wise in the way you act toward outsiders" and "that your daily life may win the respect of outsiders."[26] If this is required of Christians, how much more Christian leaders?

The apostle uses this Greek word for "good" sixteen times in 1 Timothy alone. Timothy was to fight a "*good* warfare" (1:18); deacons needed to obtain a "*good* standing" (3:13); Timothy was to be a "*good* minister" (4:6) who taught "*good* doctrine" (4:6) and fought a "*good* fight" (6:12) so he could

---

[21] See *1 & 2 Timothy & Titus*, Calvin, page 57.
[22] See Acts 10:22.
[23] See Acts 6:3.
[24] *The Pastoral Epistles*, Guthrie, pages 94-95.
[25] *A Commentary on the Pastoral Epistles*, Kelly, pages 79-80.
[26] See Colossians 4:5 and 1 Thessalonians 4:12.

maintain a "*good* confession" (6:12); Jesus also maintained this "*good* confession" (6:13) before "Pontius Pilate;" and Christians were to secure a "*good* foundation" (6:19) for the future. "Widows" (5:10), "believers" (5:25), and "rich Christians" (6:18) were to do "*good* works." Yes, "If a man desires the position of a bishop, he desires a *good* work" (3:1). He is simply following "the *good* shepherd who gives His life for the sheep."[27]

If an elder is appointed who doesn't have this type of testimony, he will "fall into" accusation, blame, criticism, and disgrace. He will also fall into the "snare" or "trap" of the devil. Paul will use this word again in a few chapters when he writes, "those who desire to be rich fall into temptation and a *snare*" and in 2 Timothy when speaking of those under Satan's bondage – "...that they may come to their senses and escape the *snare* of the devil, having been taken captive by him to do his will."[28] How can we expect this elder to lead others into the freedom of Christ when he himself is held captive by the devil because of his bad testimony? Strauch reveals the potential danger: "A man's image before his Christian brethren must not be different than his image at work, in the family, or in the neighborhood. People judge the community by its leaders. The real test of a man's character, then, is from Monday to Saturday, not on Sunday morning."[29]

Let's speak of some practical aspects of this requirement.
To maintain a good reputation with outsiders, make sure your finances are in order. Don't get into credit card debt. Pay all your bills on time. Do you have any unpaid tickets or traffic fines? Do you owe back taxes or insurance claims? Have you borrowed money from a friend? If you owe anyone money, pay it off right away. "Let no debt remain outstanding" was Paul's instruction. Jesus said in Luke 16:11, "And if you are untrustworthy about worldly wealth, who will trust you with the true riches of heaven?"

How an elder handles his personal finances will be the way he handles the church's finances. I would review a potential

---

[27] See John 10:11.
[28] See 1 Timothy 6:9 and 2 Timothy 2:26.
[29] *Biblical Eldership*, Strauch, page 204.

elder's personal finances before I put him into a leadership role. As Paul said two verses earlier, "If a man does not know how to rule his own house, how will he take care of the church of God?"

To maintain a good reputation with outsiders, make sure you are a good and hard worker in your place of employment. Colossians 3:22-23 read, "Servants, obey your earthly masters in everything you do. Try to please them all the time, not just when they are watching you. Serve them sincerely because of your reverent fear of the Lord. Work willingly at whatever you do, as though you were working for the Lord rather than for men." Always show up to work on time. Those who are consistently late have a bad reputation. Are you a man of integrity? Does your boss trust you with company assets and personnel? Would you invite your boss to church to hear you preach a sermon? Does he respect you? Have you been faithful to the same company for many years? So many Christians are unstable and move around from job to job, never able to settle down.

To maintain a good reputation with outsiders, make sure you are a man of your word. Let your "yes" be "yes" and your "no," "no." When you tell someone you're going to be somewhere at a certain time, show up early. Don't leave people waiting. Ed Cole once wrote: "A man's name is only as good as his word. His word is only as good as his character. You can tell a man's character by his words. Our word, when given, is a source of faith to those who receive it, and determines their conduct. When the word is not kept, unbelief develops. Being a man of honor is being a man of your word."[30] David wrote that the man who dwells in God's tabernacle and fears God is the one "who keeps his oath even when it hurts" or "keep their promises, no matter what the cost."[31] When you keep your word, people develop trust in you. The reason we trust God is because He always keeps His word.

I remember going to a meeting in the 1980s when Ed Cole was speaking in Columbus, Ohio. Around fifty pastors and Christian leaders signed up for the seminar. He rented a hotel

---

[30] *Communication, Sex & Money*, Edwin Louis Cole, Albury Publishing, Tulsa, Oklahoma, pages 28-29.
[31] See Psalm 15:4.

room and provided a free lunch. I drove about one hour to get to the meeting. When the meeting started only about half of these ministers showed up. They ended up throwing away a lot of food that day. Dr. Cole opened his remarks that day speaking of keeping your word. It was embarrassing that Christian leaders who name the name of Christ have a reputation of not keeping their promises. They can't be trusted.

To maintain a good reputation with outsiders, make sure you keep good relations with your immediate and extended family. What do your aunts, uncles, cousins, nieces, and nephews think of you? Are you a servant to your own family? Do you treat them well? Do they come to you for counsel and help when they have problems? Do your in-laws speak well of you?

You have been blessed to be a blessing. Let us serve our family well. They see us day by day and they know if we are people of integrity, faithfulness, and servanthood.

May outsiders endorse your desire to be an overseer in God's house. It is a good work only for good men.

3

The Church Leader Must Be of Good Behavior

"A bishop then must be blameless, the husband of
*one wife, temperate, sober-minded, **of good behavior**,*
hospitable, able to teach."
(1 Timothy 3:2)

Many years ago, I was hired as the supervisor of the administrative support staff and the computer department of a California state medical company. I worked in the main headquarters here in Fresno. The company had about 175 employees. The Chief Executive Officer (CEO) was a man named David Riester. He was an amazing leader. I learned so much from him by how he conducted himself day by day. I was friends with his executive secretary because she was a Christian believer and the editor of my teaching newsletters. She told me how he directed the company and how he did his work as the CEO.

He was always one of the first ones to arrive each morning for work, and he always wore a suit and tie. When I first walked into his large office, I noticed right away that his desk was immaculate. In a company that used many hundreds of pieces of paper every day, I never saw one paper on his desk. Why? Because each day he finished all of his work. He never left anything for the next day. Mr. Riester never procrastinated. In fact, anything that came to him – phone call, letter, message, or task – was done right then and there. For a busy executive, I was amazed that he took every phone call that came to him. His in-box was always empty at the end of each day. He was very disciplined and meticulous. He was like a well-oiled and smooth-running machine. He never seemed to be disturbed or worried. Everything about his work life seemed to be neatly arranged and organized.

David Riester is the epitome of the Greek word Paul used in 1 Timothy 3:2 for "good behavior."[32] It is the single Greek adjective, "kosimos," which comes from the well-known word, "kosmos," or where we get the English word, "cosmos." The "cosmos" means "an orderly arrangement" or an "orderly system or universe." It is any system that is an integrated whole or a harmonious unit that works together in an orderly fashion. One paraphrase version of 1 Timothy 3:2 uses "orderly" and others use "respectable," "respected by others," "well-behaved," and "has a good reputation." Stott says "it is the outward expression of an inward self-control."[33]

The elder must be a person whose personal and spiritual life is organized and orderly. He must be a leader whose life is in order. Any machine that is "out of order" does not work and cannot be used. Kelly defines "kosimos" as "dignified" which emphasizes "the overseer's external deportment."[34] He refers to the manner in which a person behaves or conducts himself. Barclay writes that "kosimos" speaks of good "outward behavior," then adds, "This word has more in it than simply good behavior. It describes the person whose life is beautiful and in whose character all things are harmoniously integrated."[35]

When I think of someone in the Bible who was "kosimos," I think of the prophet Daniel. This is an amazing

---

[32] The only other appearance of this word in the New Testament is a few verses earlier in 1 Timothy 2:9, where Paul said that women must wear "*modest* apparel."

[33] *The Message of 1 Timothy & Titus*, Stott, page 95.

[34] *A Commentary on the Pastoral Epistles*, Kelly, page 76. Mounce defines it as "decent or dignified which refers to a person's outward deportment or outward appearance" (page 173).

[35] *The Letters to Timothy, Titus, and Philemon*, William Barclay, The New Daily Study Bible, Westminster John Knox Press, pages 90-91.

statement about him – "Then this Daniel distinguished himself above the governors and satraps, because an excellent spirit was in him; and the king gave thought to setting him over the whole realm. So the governors and satraps sought to find some charge against Daniel concerning the kingdom; but they could find no charge or fault, because he was faithful; nor was there any error or fault found in him" (6:3-4). What an amazing testimony! Three governors and 120 rulers (satraps) in the entire Babylonian kingdom looked for something wrong in Daniel's conduct of government affairs and they found nothing! No one in today's government has that kind of spotless record.

The Christian leader is doing a "good work" (3:1), so he must be of "good behavior" (3:2) with a "good reputation with outsiders" (3:7). He must be "a lover of good things" (Titus 1:8). Then "you will be a good minister of Jesus Christ who carefully follows good doctrine." The elder is a good leader.

As I move into speaking about the practical application of this quality (kosimos), I'd like to use Yarbrough's definition of the word. He writes, "The sense is having characteristics or qualities that evoke admiration or delight, so that the person is held in high regard. Paul wants overseers whose characteristic actions cause them to be held in high esteem."[36] If people in your congregation don't respect the way you look, dress, behave, and conduct yourself outside of church, what makes you think they will respect what you say on Sunday morning? Though it may come across carnal, your social and physical bearing must translate into a lifestyle that earns the respect of others.

Let's start with your personal and home life. *Keep your house, car, and personal appearance neat and orderly.* Is the inside of your car or truck full of trash? Is your vehicle unkempt and dirty? Many years ago, an elderly pastoral supervisor told us younger pastors that he could qualify or disqualify a candidate for ministry by just looking at the inside of his car. He said that a messy and neglected car speaks volumes about a person's character. Remember: You are charged with overseeing people's

---

[36] *The Letters to Timothy and Titus*, Robert W. Yarbrough, The Pillar New Testament Commentary, Eerdmans Publishing, page 196.

souls; if you can't even keep your car clean, what makes you think you will help others live a virtuous life?!

I thank the Lord that my wife likes to keep a clean house. She is very diligent to make sure the kitchen, living room, bathrooms, and bedrooms are clean. Her cleanliness keeps me on my toes. What does the front of your house look like? And what about your garage? A disordered house communicates to others a disordered life.

In today's world of pastors and church leaders, they have little regard for their physical appearance. So many elders and bishops are overweight and dress inappropriately. This is the new standard – torn jeans, old shoes, sweat pants, and clothes that are not clean. This "outward adornment" will not garner respect. This is not dignified. You are representing Christ and His kingdom.

Keep the church facilities neat and orderly. The area around the altar and pulpit should be very clean and presentable. Everyone, including the visitors, will notice a messy front stage. The church elder wants the sanctuary, restrooms, and classrooms clean and neatly arranged. I've been to church facilities where the bathrooms are dirty and trash cans are overflowing. This is not good.

Have you ever inspected a sanctuary on Monday morning? People leave bulletins, water bottles, notes, tissue, and even their Bibles on chairs, pews, and the floor. I call them "sheep droppings!" And so many believers never bother to pick anything up when they see it. They just step right over things and keep on going. They don't take any pride of ownership in their church building or church grounds.

Again, don't assume all of this is carnal. It says a lot about the leadership of the church.

Have you noticed how orderly the Lord was with the tabernacle of Moses and the tribes of Israel in the wilderness? When the Israelite camp had to move, they blew the shofar and the tribes went out in a very specific order one after another (in groups of three), first from the east, then the south, then the north, and finally, the west. The furniture was assembled and disassembled in a very careful order. The priests were very careful about every function in the Holy Place and with the furniture pieces and sacrifices outside. The high priest was especially careful when he went into the Holy of Holies once a year on the Day of Atonement. They did not move randomly or by some independent method. No, God's house should be a house of order. They followed an orderly procedure.

When describing the conduct and order of church services and how the gifts of the Spirit should operate when God's people gather together, Paul wrote, "For God is not the author of confusion but of peace, as in all the churches of the saints. Let all things be done decently and in order."[37]

As church elders and overseers, we must keep the services orderly and well-behaved. The church leader has his hand on the pulse of each service. We notice when the spiritual atmosphere is down and depressed; we notice when things are getting out of control. If something is wrong or inappropriate, stand up and correct it. Provide leadership. If someone is getting out of hand emotionally or starts disrupting the service, work with the ushers to gently move them to another room or outside the service. If some part of the service is taking too long, then take the microphone and move things forward. *All things* must be done "decently and in order."

I remember once when a lady came to the front of the church to receive prayer. She had just gone through something very traumatic in her marriage and family. She began to speak out hysterically and shaking uncontrollably. Nearly everyone stopped worshipping and the worship team stopped playing. I quickly stood up, called several leaders to get around her to pray, and then I went over to her and prayed words of peace while laying hands on her head. She immediately calmed down and the service resumed.

Exodus 32:25 says, "Moses saw that the people were unrestrained (for Aaron had not restrained them, to their shame among their enemies)." Don't let things get out of control.

Another time, we were singing some beautiful and powerful songs about the love of God and the sacrifice of Jesus on the cross, and the church service was spiritually dead. After the second song, I had to stand up and exhort the congregation to awaken from its slumber and remember why we were there that

---

[37] See 1 Corinthians 14:33 and 14:40.

morning. At other times, some of the songs spoke to us about victory and deliverance, and those were times to call people forth for prayer or repentance. The church elder follows the leading of the Holy Spirit and establishes the setting whereby God's people can receive healing and a touch from the Lord.

This is very much a part of "behaving well" and leading a church into "good behavior."

In the next chapter, let's continue this theme of "good things." The church leader must be "a lover of good things."

4

The Church Leader Must Be a Lover of Good Things

*"For a bishop must be hospitable, **a lover of what is good**, sober-minded, just, holy, self-controlled."*
(Titus 1:8)

One of the main attributes of God is that "He is good." On Mount Sinai, Moses heard the Lord proclaim that "He is abounding in goodness and truth." When God's people began to praise and worship Him, they shouted, "Oh, give thanks to the Lord, for He is good! For His mercy endures forever!" David said, "The Lord is good to all," and Asaph his worship leader said, "Truly God is good to Israel."

It is in the Psalms where the Lord's goodness is magnified: "Good and upright is the Lord," "Oh, how great is Your goodness," "the earth is full of the goodness of the Lord," "Oh, taste and see that the Lord is good," "the goodness of God endures continually," "for You, Lord, are good, and ready to forgive," "Oh, that men would give thanks to the Lord for His goodness," and "praise the Lord, for the Lord is good."[38]

It should go without saying that an elder's life and character should reflect the nature of the God who is good.

The Greek word Paul used in Titus 1:8 for "a lover of what is good" is a single, compound adjective, "philagathos." It

---

[38] Psalm 25:8, 31:19, 33:5, 34:8, 52:1, 86:5, 107:8, and 135:3.

literally means "good-loving" from "philo" = to be fond of; like; love + "agathos" = good. It appears only here in the New Testament and nowhere else. The elder must be a "lover of strangers" (*philo*xenos) and a "lover of good" (*phila*gathos), but not a "lover of silver" (*aphila*rguros). Like Barnabas and Joseph of Arimathea, the church leader must be a "good man."[39]

Various commentators define "philagathos" as "devotion to all that is best," "one who is devoted to kindness," "a supporter of all good causes," "devoted to things that promote good," and "zealous to see that what is good flourishes in and out of the church."[40] Knight gives us the right perspective. "An overseer's love for people is always to be correlated with a love for what God wants people to be."[41]

The word "good" and its related forms appears nearly 800 times in the Bible. It is one of the major character themes of Scripture. "Goodness" is a fruit of the Spirit. All Christians are to "cling to what is good," "say what is good to build others up," "turn away from evil and do good," and "do good to all, especially those who are of the household of faith."[42] We are exhorted "not to forget to do good and to share, for with such sacrifices God is well pleased," and John reminds us, "Beloved, do not imitate what is evil, but what is good. He who does good is of God." The only One who is good, Jesus, "went about doing good and healing all who were oppressed by the devil."[43]

You can tell a "good elder" by the fruit of his life. Jesus said, "You will know them by their fruits. Every good tree bears good fruit, but a bad tree bears bad fruit." He also said, "A good man out of the good treasure of his heart brings forth good things." On the last day, we want the Lord to tell us, "Well done, good and faithful servant."[44]

---

[39] See Acts 11:24 and Luke 23:50.

[40] Kelly (page 232); Calvin (page 184); Stott (page 177); Towner (page 227); Yarbrough (page 486).

[41] *The Pastoral Epistles*, George W. Knight III, The New International Greek Testament Commentary, Eerdmans Publishing, page 292.

[42] See Galatians 5:22; Ephesians 5:9; Romans 12:9; Ephesians 4:29; Galatians 6:10; 1 Peter 3:11.

[43] See Hebrews 13:16; 3 John 11; Acts 10:38.

[44] See Matthew 7:16-17, 12:35, 25:21, and 25:23.

Here are a few practical considerations for the church leader who is "a lover of what is good."

The church elder will love and keep a close eye on children and widows. His heart will be concerned for the elderly of the church.

James 1:27 reads, "Pure and undefiled religion before God and the Father is this: to visit orphans and widows in their trouble, and to keep oneself unspotted from the world." Most local churches in the United States (80%) are under 200 people. I would make it a point to know the names of all the children and teenagers in your congregation. As much as possible, greet them at each service by name. Engage them. Talk to them. Let them know that they are seen and appreciated.

I have attended nearly all the high school graduations and special birthdays of anyone in our youth group, especially if they have invited me. This is an important time to connect with them and show them support. The pastor's presence is so important to families when they are honoring significant milestones in the life of their children.

The elderly in the church are some of the most faithful and committed believers. They must never be overlooked. In many churches, 50-60% of the finances are coming from those who are considered seniors. Many of them are faithful prayer warriors. Over the years, I have recruited many of them to be my personal intercessors.

I'll never forget what an elderly man in our church told me years ago. He said, "Pastor, I feel very reassured that when I go home to be with the Lord, this local church will look out for my wife. I see how everyone here rallies around the widows of the church. I'll be at peace when I check out."

Call the seniors or widows of your church every month. Greet them at every church service. Ask them about their health. So many are struggling with health issues. Yes, their immediate family has primary responsibility for their overall care,[45] but we

---

[45] 1 Timothy 5:16 – "If any believing man or woman has widows, let them relieve them, and do not let the church be burdened, that it may relieve those who are really widows."

must always acknowledge them and make sure they are being watched.

The church elder will look for and highlight the good things he sees in other people. One author writes, "The Christian elder must be someone whose heart answers to the good in whatever person, wherever and in whatever circumstances it is found."[46] There's an old adage in the ministry: *If you look for dirt, you'll be sure to find it.* Everyone can see the character flaws in others. Everyone can magnify the negative things in marriages and families. It takes a man of courage and truth to see the good in others. It's actually a very challenging task. We live in a church world that is very pessimistic.

Before and after church services are great times to acknowledge and edify faithful workers in your church. Go to that Sunday School teacher before the service as she's setting up her classroom and let her know that you and the church appreciate her time and commitment. After the service, walk up to that person who is a faithful usher and thank him for the good work he is doing. Talk to that worship singer and let him know that his worshipful attitude and singing voice blesses you. Write people short notes in cards and give it to them. I remember one year, I wrote a short note each week to a different person in our church thanking them for all they do for the Lord and His church. I was amazed at how many times this lit up the countenance of these good people. *Point out the good in others.*

Is it not sad that one of the times when we thank and acknowledge someone the most is at their funeral, but they're not around to hear any of it?!

Elders should possess a ministry of encouragement. It is so vital and so needed today. Have you ever seen how often that word appears in the New Testament?

There is a motivational gift of encouragement: "If it is encouraging, let him encourage." Prophecy is a gift that "speaks to men for their strengthening, encouragement and comfort." Paul wrote many words of encouragement to individuals and to churches. Sometimes he even sent people to different locations just to encourage others: "My purpose is that they may be

---

[46] *The Letters to Timothy, Titus, and Philemon*, Barclay, page 268.

encouraged in heart and united in love," "I am sending him (Tychicus) to you for the express purpose that he may encourage your hearts," "we were encouraging, comforting and urging you to live lives worthy of God," "we sent Timothy...to strengthen and encourage you in your faith," "therefore encourage each other with these words," "encourage one another and build each other up, just as in fact you are doing," "encourage the timid," "so that he (the elder) can encourage others by sound doctrine," "encourage the young men to be self-controlled," "encourage and rebuke with all authority," "encourage one another daily, as long as it is called Today," and "let us encourage one another – and all the more as you see the Day approaching."[47] Yes, the Word of God says much about encouragement. And the New Testament overseer must encourage his flock.

Barnabas (which means Son of Encouragement), "encouraged them all to remain true to the Lord with all their hearts." The early church prophets were not just speaking prophetic words over people, they were encouraging believers: "Judas and Silas, who themselves were prophets, said much to encourage and strengthen the brothers."[48]

The church elder will support church, local, and national issues that promote family health and family values. One of my favorite verses on marriage is Hebrews 13:4. It begins with the words, "Marriage should be honored by all." Everyone should honor marriage. Incorporate into the life of your local church the honoring of married couples who celebrate milestones, especially 25, 50, and 60-year anniversaries. In every possible way, support local Pregnancy Care Centers and pro-life movements. Speak out against homosexual marriages, transgender policies, and divorce. Encourage Christians to adopt children, homeschool, and be positive influences for good in the community. My wife and I have done all of these things. It's amazing what your example will do to other families in the church.

---

[47] See the NIV translation of Romans 12:8; 1 Corinthians 14:3; Colossians 2:2, 4:8; 1 Thessalonians 2:12, 3:2, 4:18, 5:11, 5:14; Titus 1:9, 2:6, 2:15; Hebrews 3:13, 10:25.
[48] See Acts 4:36, 11:23, and 15:32.

5

The Church Leader Must Be Hospitable

*"A bishop then must be blameless, the husband of one wife, temperate, sober-minded, of good behavior, **hospitable**, able to teach."*
(1 Timothy 3:2)

*"For a bishop must be **hospitable**, a lover of what is good, sober-minded, just, holy, self-controlled."*
(Titus 1:8)

There is nothing more attractive, appealing, positive, and winsome than a church and its leaders who reach out and greet, embrace, and welcome new people and visitors. This is the very definition of "hospitality" or "to be hospitable" – "friendly, welcoming, and generous to guests or strangers." It comes from an old French word, "hospiter,"[49] which means, "receive a guest."

The Greek word Paul used in 1 Timothy 3:2 and Titus 1:8 for "hospitable" has the same definition. "Philoxenos" is a compound word that literally means "philo" = to be fond of; like; love + "xenos" = a stranger. I really like the wording of various modern translations – "He must enjoy having guests in his home,"

---

[49] It is interesting that "hospital" is derived from this word. "Hospitals" are places where sick "guests" are treated with care.

"he must be ready to help people by welcoming them into his home," "friendly to strangers," and "ready to welcome guests." The old KJV of Titus 1:8 has "...a lover of hospitality."

Jesus' famous words in Matthew 25 are pertinent: "I was a stranger (Greek, xenos) and you took Me in" (v35). They asked the Lord, "When did we see You a stranger (xenos) and take You in, or naked and clothe You?" Jesus responded, "Assuredly, I say to you, inasmuch as you did it to one of the least of these My brethren, you did it to Me" (v40).[50] Amazingly, those who did not welcome strangers and take them in, not only did not receive Christ, but they eventually were cast into the everlasting fire! Pretty serious indeed!

The apostle John commended the brothers who faithfully "cared for traveling teachers who pass through, even though they are strangers (xenos) to you."[51] Christians were taking care of the needs of these strangers even though they didn't know them. All they did know was that they were preaching the gospel, and to help these teachers was to participate directly in the blessings and rewards of their work.

We need to be aware that when we do "entertain" certain people, we may actually be hosting angels! Hebrews 13:2 reads, "Don't forget to *show hospitality to strangers*, for some who have done this have entertained angels without realizing it!" The Greek word the writer of Hebrews used here is nearly identical to the one Paul used for elders. It is "philoxenia" and it's derived from "philoxenos." In fact, these two words are listed one after another in the New Testament Greek dictionary.

Paul commanded us to "share with God's people who are in need. Practice hospitality." One translation ends with "always be eager to practice hospitality."[52] Christian widows had to be known for "lodging strangers (xenos)"[53] or literally "receiving strangers." The apostle Peter warned us, "Be hospitable to one

---

[50] Compare with John 13:20, "Most assuredly, I say to you, he who receives whomever I send receives Me; and he who receives Me receives Him who sent Me."

[51] See 3 John 5.

[52] See Romans 12:13.

[53] See 1 Timothy 5:10.

another without grumbling."[54]   Sometimes showing hospitality can move you out of your comfort zone and cause you to deny yourself. Selfish people are not hospitable. It's easy to complain, murmur, and grumble. Consider it a privilege when God uses you to bless others.

Today, when guest speakers come to our churches, we usually put them up in a local hotel and they never see our homes. However, in New Testament times, inns were often dirty, seedy, and even dangerous. The necessity of opening our homes to traveling ministers or out of town visitors was obligatory. Towner's comments are very insightful: "This widely praised virtue in that day was practically a social obligation for the householder. It became a mark of Christian behavior. What sometimes passes for hospitality today (the entertainment of friends and church members, often with the expectation of a return invitation) is a rather dim reflection of the New Testament concept. The practice of hospitality among Christians was often urgent, sacrificial, and risky: urgent because Christians might be forced from homes or jobs with no one to turn to but fellow Christians; sacrificial because material goods were often in short supply; risky because to associate oneself with those who had been forced out meant to identify with their cause. Thus, hospitality required sacrificial sharing and stretching. It was a very practical expression of love, not a source of entertainment. While the practice of hospitality had primarily the needs of believers in mind, there is no reason that it could not be a way of showing concern for unbelievers. The importance of this practice for the church, in either case, required that a leader must model it for all."[55] The elder must be hospitable.

What are some practical things a church elder can do to show hospitality to believers and strangers?

Go out of your way to greet visitors. For various reasons, so many church members walk right past people who are visiting the church for the first time and don't even greet them. The church

---

[54] See 1 Peter 4:9. Besides 1 Timothy 3:2 and Titus 1:8, this is the only other place in the New Testament where the word, "philoxenos," is used.
[55] *1-2 Timothy & Titus*, Philip H. Towner, The IVP New Testament Commentary Series, Inter-Varsity Press, page 227.

elder always goes to strangers and greets them. Introduce yourself. Shake hands. Stay and talk to them for a few minutes. Don't just acknowledge them from the pulpit; greet them in person.

Many years ago, I was part of a church that invited all the new people downstairs to the basement after the church service for punch, coffee, cookies, and some snacks. We announced during the service that all visitors could go downstairs and meet with the pastors and church leaders. Why did we do this? We read statistics that indicated that visitors were seven times more likely to return to a church if they met the pastor and his leaders in person. There is something powerful about a church where the leaders know the new people by name after the first or second visit.

Invite people over to your house. "The Christian leader must be a man with an open heart and an open house."[56] Your church members will not really know you until they have been to your house. Invite them over for dinner. Bring them over for a dessert. Cook a few hamburgers and hot dogs and sit down in the backyard for a few hours. It's amazing the connection you can make with people after spending 3-4 hours with them at your house. Jesus said that taking in strangers was just like taking Him in. That's pretty significant!

The people in the church that I'm closest to are those who have spent the most time at my house. They not only know *where* I live, they also know *how* I live. Your home defines the way you live your life.

Take new people out to eat after church services. My wife and I have made it a point to take visitors out to eat at a local restaurant after their third or fourth visit. Nothing solidifies the connection with new people like taking them out to eat and paying for their meal. Nearly all the new people who have joined our church in the last few years went to lunch with us after a Sunday service.

Every bishop, elder, and pastor should be against that church leader who finishes his Sunday sermon and then escapes through some side door. Most leaders of large churches rarely

---

[56] *The Letters to Timothy, Titus, and Philemon*, Barclay, page 91.

interact with their congregations. Strauch writes, "A man who closes his door to God's family cannot be an elder. Indeed, such action is symptomatic of more serious problems. Lack of hospitality among the Lord's people is a sure sign of selfish, lifeless, loveless Christianity."[57]

Leaders must engage people regularly. The heart of the shepherding ministry is John 10:14, "I am the good shepherd; I know My sheep and My sheep know Me." Good shepherds know the sheep and the sheep know them. People will not really know you if you don't spend time with them.

---

[57] *Biblical Eldership*, Strauch, page 197.

6

The Church Leader Must Be Temperate

*"A bishop then must be blameless, the husband of one wife, **temperate**, sober-minded, of good behavior, hospitable, able to teach."*
(1 Timothy 3:2)

The principal author of the Declaration of Independence and the third president of the United States was Thomas Jefferson. He once wrote, "Nothing gives one person so much advantage over another as to remain always cool and unruffled under all circumstances." Dr. John Maxwell, the Christian leadership trainer and speaker, once said, "A leader must be able to concentrate under difficult conditions – to keep his head when all others about him are losing theirs."[58] These are good definitions of the word, "temperate."

The dictionary defines "temperate" as "mild or restrained in behavior or attitude." In the world of meteorology, we hear of "temperate climate," which means any climate "without extremes" or one where the temperatures stay within "moderate limits." I recently went to a ministers' conference in Medellin, Colombia. It is a city that is near the equator. It is known as "the

---

[58] Both quotes taken from *Leadership 101*, John C. Maxwell, Inspirational Quotes & Insights for Leaders, Honor Books, Tulsa, Oklahoma, pages 45 and 65.

city of eternal springs" because the average temperature year-round is a mild 72F.

The Greek word Paul used in 1 Timothy 3:2, "nēphaleos," means "sober; circumspect; discreet." He will use it again in 1 Timothy 3:11 as a qualification for the deacon's wife, "…their wives must be reverent, not slanderers, *temperate*, faithful in all things." He also uses it in Titus 2:2 – "…the older men must be *sober*." Hiebert gives a good definition: "Literally it means 'unmixed with wine, wineless.' He is to be a man sober and fully rational, in possession of the full use of all his faculties."[59] Fee says "it is used figuratively to mean free from every form of excess, passion, or rashness."[60] Kelly translates the word, "clear-minded."[61]

In this chapter and the next two, we will study three qualifications that have roughly the same meaning. Elders must be "temperate," "sober-minded," and "self-controlled." The elder must not be given to extremes. He must be balanced, consistent, mild, and steady. Stott says these qualities are part of the elder's "self-mastery."[62] Can he master himself? We'll see why later on, Paul will require elders to not be quarrelsome, violent, and soon angry. The elder must be level-headed.

When Paul was teaching in 1 Corinthians 9:24-27 on how Christians are running a race and we need to run in such a way to win the prize, he states that "everyone who competes for the prize is *temperate* in all things" (v25). This means that the athlete (and the Christian) must be disciplined and self-controlled.

As a church leader, you will confront many, many situations and people who are angry, bitter, offended, irritated, and indignant. The elder must remain calm. He must use Proverbs 15:1, "A gentle answer turns away wrath, but a harsh word stirs up anger." Elders need to know how to calm people down.

---

[59] *First Timothy*, Hiebert, page 65.

[60] *1 and 2 Timothy, Titus*, Gordon D. Fee, New International Biblical Commentary, Hendrickson Publishers, page 81.

[61] *A Commentary on the Pastoral Epistles*, Kelly, page 76. Knight uses "sober in the sense of clear-headed, self-controlled," page 159.

[62] *The Message of 1 Timothy & Titus*, Stott, page 94.

I think of the story of Moses in Numbers 20 when the people's disobedience made him so angry that he yelled at them, "You rebels!" He struck the rock twice in anger and he ended up forfeiting his place in the Promised Land. Over and over again, the Israelites angered Moses. Psalm 106:32-33 summarizes well what happened to him in the wilderness: "They angered Him also at the waters of strife, so that it went ill with Moses on account of them; because they rebelled against His Spirit, so that he spoke rashly with his lips."

Over the years, Christians have called me "a shark," "modern-day Pharisee," "Job's friend," "the worthless shepherd" (Zechariah 11), and many other colorful words that cannot be repeated in this book. One young man came to our church and pronounced curses and doom when he found out that we didn't observe the Saturday Sabbath. We had to escort him out of the building. One wife told me that every day her husband was getting high using marijuana in the backyard of their house. Another man was beating his wife physically nearly every day when he got home from work. One of the ladies in our church stood up in the middle of a Wednesday night service and said, "You don't practice what you preach. I don't believe you!" That was a fun service!

I've encountered angry and tense situations at funerals, weddings, and counseling sessions. Many Christians are not calm or mild. They are on edge. They are ready to explode. The elder must be temperate. Strauch says, "It is absolutely essential that a Christian leader who faces many serious problems, pressures, and decisions be a spiritually stable man." He defines "nēphaleos" as "mental, behavioral, and spiritual sobriety."[63]

I officiated a funeral one time for a relative of mine. Her dad had just passed away. The dad had two brothers. All three men were in their seventies. *They were bitter enemies and they had not spoken to each other in decades.* I had to work with the family to allow one brother to see the body and leave, and then the other brother would come sometime later. They couldn't be in the same room because the family feared a fight might break out. The day of the actual funeral was tense. One brother came in early and

---

[63] *Biblical Eldership*, Strauch, pages 195-196.

sat in the front; the other brother came in late and sat in the back. I had to stay calm and help my relative to stay calm and talked to these two brothers to stay calm. The elder must be temperate! You cannot allow their anger to make you angry.

About fifteen years ago, I officiated a wedding in the backyard of a close friend. The couple was in love and a lot of beautiful and flowery words were exchanged.

Fast-forward about ten years later, the couple was now living in separate homes. The wife had not divorced her husband but she now had a boyfriend. Unfortunately, the wife died of an unknown illness while living with him.

At the funeral, the boyfriend stayed in front of the casket crying up a storm and kissing the face of the deceased girlfriend for nearly one hour. The husband became very angry because he had to wait outside the funeral home until the boyfriend left. The tension was nearly unbearable. I had to speak to both men in a calm voice and arrange for each man to go in at separate times. That whole service was full of stress for the family and friends. The elder must be temperate!

If someone in the church has made me angry, I've learned to go immediately to the church sanctuary and pray. I need to calm down. I can't let what they have said or done to get into my heart and mind. I know I'm going to say words that I will deeply regret later. I need the Holy Spirit to restrain me.

Let's continue this theme in the next chapter and speak of the church leader being "sober-minded."

7

The Church Leader Must Be
Sober-Minded

*"A bishop then must be blameless, the husband of
one wife, temperate, **sober-minded**, of good behavior,
hospitable, able to teach."*
(1 Timothy 3:2)

*"For a bishop must be hospitable, a lover of what is
good, **sober-minded**, just, holy, self-controlled."*
(Titus 1:8)

The statistics are tragic: Alcohol is the number one drug problem in America. Between twelve to fifteen million people in this country are alcoholics. In the United States, a person is killed in an alcohol-related car accident every thirty minutes, which amounts to nearly half of all fatal car crashes. Last year, over one million drivers were arrested for "driving under the influence" (DUI). Americans spend $197 million *each day* on alcohol without considering that more than 100,000 deaths occur annually due to excessive alcohol consumption. That works out to 274 people every single day. Three-fourths of all high school seniors report being drunk at least once. And it is an interesting fact that people with higher education and higher income are more likely to drink and abuse alcohol. Just because you know more, doesn't mean you live better.

The statistics on alcoholics listed above do not include the "other victims" – those affected by alcohol though they are not alcoholics and may not even drink at all. Consider that alcohol is a factor in the following: 73% of all felonies, 73% of child beatings, 41% of rape cases, 81% of wife battering cases, 72% of stabbings, and 83% of homicides.

In a recent study, 3.3 million deaths, or 5.9 percent of all global deaths (7.6 percent for men and 4.0 percent for women), were attributable to alcohol consumption. Alcohol contributes to over 200 diseases and injury-related health conditions, most notably alcohol dependence, liver cirrhosis, cancers, and injuries. Globally, alcohol misuse is the fifth leading risk factor for premature death and disability. Among people between the ages of 15 and 49, it is the first.[64]

Before Christ Jesus delivered me from my sins and rebellion, I drank a lot. In this drunken environment, I came to understand the term "be sober" or "to sober up." It meant to not be intoxicated. It meant that you were no longer under the influence of alcohol. When you are sober, you return to reality and you can face the day with a clear mind and rational thinking. To be sober was to be in control of all your faculties and reasoning. You could walk without falling, drive without crashing, and talk without slurring. To be sober was to be in your right mind.

The apostles of Jesus Christ commanded Christians to be sober, but it was not a physical sobriety, but a spiritual one. Peter said, "Be sober" and "be sober-minded;" Paul taught to "be sober," "live soberly," and "think soberly." To be sober is to be alert and awake. You cannot be asleep. You must be vigilant and watchful. You cannot be "under the influence" of the flesh, the world, and the devil. The sober Christian is fully aware that the Day of the Lord is coming, so he must get himself ready; that the devil is seeking whom he may devour, so Christians must be on guard; that ungodliness and worldly lusts/passions are all around us, so Christians must deny the alluring desires of the flesh. To be sober is to be under the influence of the Word of God and the

---

[64] This statistic information is readily available from groups such as the National Council on Alcohol, National Institute of Alcohol Abuse and Alcoholism (NIAAA), National Highway Traffic Safety Administration (NHTSA), and the American Automobile Association (AAA).

Spirit of God. Sober Christians are not drunk with the maddening wine of the Babylonian prostitute.[65]

Paul told Timothy and Titus that "bishops" and "elders" must be "sober-minded." The Greek adjective that Paul uses, "sōphrona," is a compound word that means "sound + mind" or "healthy + thinking." There is a particular emphasis on the way the person thinks. Such a leader is discreet, temperate, and self-restrained. He is not given to extremes or wild conclusions.

The New Testament uses six different variations of "sōphrona" as verbs, adverbs, adjectives, and nouns. When Jesus delivered the Gadarene demoniac from the "legion" of demons, they found him "sitting and clothed and in his *right mind* (sōphronounta)."[66] He was now sane. Paul used the same verb in Titus 2:6 – "Exhort the young men to be *sober-minded* (sōphronein)." Older women were to teach younger women "to be *sober*" (sōphronizō) so they could "be *discreet*" (sōphrōn) in Titus 2:4-5. The apostle told Timothy that "God has not given us a spirit of fear, but of power and of love and of a *sound mind*" (sōphronismou).[67] "The grace of God that brings salvation has appeared to all men, teaching us that, denying ungodliness and worldly lusts, we should *live soberly* (sōphronōs), righteously, and godly in the present age."[68] In 1 Timothy 2:9, Paul says "that the women should adorn themselves in modest apparel, with propriety and *moderation* (sōphrosunēs), not with braided hair or gold or pearls or costly clothing." The word is rendered "sensible" and "self-controlled" in other translations. He uses the word again a few verses later when he writes, "She will be saved in childbearing if she continues in faith, love, and holiness with *self-control* (sōphrosunēs)" (2:15). The same word used of bishops and elders is required of "old men": "That the older men *be sober* (sōphronas), reverent, temperate, sound in faith, in love, in patience."[69]

These words reveal that to be "sober-minded" is someone in his right mind, who thinks soberly, and lives a life of sobriety,

---

[65] See the wording of Revelation 14:3, 17:2, and 18:3.
[66] See Mark 5:15; Luke 8:35.
[67] See 2 Timothy 1:7.
[68] See Titus 2:11-12.
[69] See Titus 2:2.

self-control, and moderate thinking. The bottom line is the elder has a good head on his shoulders.

Church leaders are going to make decisions, give counsel, and teach others on a regular basis. They will face life and death situations. The leader must be level-headed, secure, and trusted. He cannot be given to irrational thinking. Church members are already dealing with a lot of chaos and drama; they cannot have more confusion from bad advice.

Let me give briefly three considerations on "sober thinking" for elders.

Paul wrote in Romans 12:3, "For I say to everyone who is among you, not to think of himself more highly than he ought to think, but *to think soberly* (sōphronein) as God has dealt to each one a measure of faith."

As I meditated one day on Romans 12, I began to see clearly the power and truth of Paul's words about being truly sober before God and His people. How this teaching is needed in the body of Christ today! Too many Christian leaders have a completely wrong estimation of themselves, their gifts, their capabilities, and their ministries. Like the man who has had too much alcohol or drugs, too many leaders today are "high on themselves." Paul said, "Do not think more *highly* than you ought" and "do not set your mind on *high* things" (12:16). We must go "low," or as Paul says, "Be willing to associate with people of *low* position" (12:16, NIV).

If you are going to think soberly, you must be fully convinced that everything you have and all that you are comes from God and His grace. Without God's grace, you would be nothing. As elders, let us not try to impress others with our knowledge, experience, and wisdom. We don't need to let people know how long we've been in leadership nor how many degrees we have. Let us become like children and humble ourselves.

I recently heard one pastor talking to another one – "I need to get our church pass the 500 mark to validate my ministry. We are packed every Sunday. We have multiple services." You could hear the pride oozing from this man's lips. What was particularly distressing was that the pastor he was talking to had just told him how his church attendance had gone down and he was discouraged about what was happening in his small church. It is terribly sad that so many pastors equate the size of their church with how gifted they are, how powerful they must be, how anointed their ministry is, or how popular their messages are. Subtly, they reason in their high-mindedness – *the bigger the church, the better the minister.* This is categorically false. The United Bible Society (UBS) translators say that Romans 12:3 could be translated as "do not think of yourselves with a big head" or "do not say to yourselves, I am so very big, when you really are not." How pastors need to humble themselves today! We are not that great. The only one who is truly great is the God whom we serve. What is really great is the grace that He gives. Again, without Jesus we could do nothing! Think soberly!

Secondly, Peter wrote in 1 Peter 4:7 (KJV), "But the end of all things is at hand: be ye therefore *sober* (sōphronēsate), and watch unto prayer." The church leader is fully aware that we are in the last days. The end is near. Because it is, we need to be sober. How can we do that? Peter gives us the answer – "be watchful in prayer." *The best way to maintain sober-thinking is to spend a lot of time in prayer.* The elder who is constant and faithful in prayer will get his direction from the Lord and his judgments and decisions will be balanced and correct.

Finally, Peter also wrote, "*Be sober*, be vigilant; because your adversary the devil walks about like a roaring lion, seeking whom he may devour."[70]

One of the main reasons we suffer is because we have an adversary. The reason Christian leaders are suffering is because the devil is seeking them. He is seeking whom he may devour. In order to continue standing against the devil, you must "be sober," "be vigilant," "resist the devil," and remain "steadfast in the faith." You do not stand idle and passive; you fight and resist in the name of Jesus. Grudem writes, "The word 'resist' implies active, determined opposition, often through confrontation."[71]

Because the devil is very active at "walking," "seeking," "roaring," and "devouring," Peter commands believers to "be

---

[70] See 1 Peter 5:8.

[71] *1 Peter,* Wayne Grudem, Tyndale New Testament Commentaries, Eerdmans Publishing, Grand Rapids, Michigan, page 197.

sober," "be vigilant," and "resist the devil."[72] Another writer commanded us in James 4:7, "Resist the devil and he will flee from you." Elders must stay alert, stay awake, and be on our guard. Bishops must be constantly ready. They must be prepared for what will happen. Peter had already told us earlier to "gird up the loins of your mind and be sober."[73]

The author of 1 Peter learned by personal experience the terrible consequences of not being sober and alert. He learned firsthand what it was like to be in the lion's mouth. Jesus told Peter in the Garden at Gethsemane to "watch and pray." He did neither. In fact, In his pride, he said, "Though everyone else will deny You, I am ready to go with You both to prison and to death."[74] But he was not ready. In his pride, he was deceived. When the test came, he crashed. He fell asleep, almost killed Malchus with the sword, and denied Jesus three times. No wonder Jesus told him, "Simon, Simon! Indeed, Satan has asked for you (plural), that he may sift you as wheat. But I have prayed for you (singular), that your (singular) faith should not fail." Peter's faith was about "to cease" or "to die." Peter was almost swallowed whole.

Church elder, be sober-minded. Think soberly. Be sober through your prayer life. Be sober-minded because the devil is seeking whom he may devour in your flock.

---

[72] These are all Greek imperative verbs of command. We *must* do these things. There are no other options.

[73] See 1 Peter 1:13.

[74] See Luke 22:33.

8

The Church Leader Must Be Self-Controlled

*"For a bishop must be hospitable, a lover of what is good, sober-minded, just, holy, **self-controlled.**"*
(Titus 1:8)

The 33rd President of the United States was Harry Truman. He was a prolific reader. He once wrote, "In reading the lives of great men, I found that the first victory they won was over themselves; that is, self-discipline with all of them came first."[75] The dictionary defines "self-control" as "self-discipline; restraint; the ability to control your own behavior, especially in terms of reactions and impulses." How are you going to bring self-control and self-discipline to a congregation if you don't even have it over yourself?

The Greek adjective for "self-controlled" (egkratēs) in Titus 1:8 is found only here in the New Testament. Its noun form appears in Galatians 5:23, "But the fruit of the Spirit is…gentleness and *self-control*. Against such there is no law."[76] Peter also used it in 2 Peter 1:5-6 when he said, "Add to your faith virtue, to virtue knowledge, to knowledge *self-control*, to *self-control* perseverance, to perseverance godliness." Paul put the

---

[75] *Leadership 101*, Maxwell, page 57.
[76] Towner says, "This observable quality is truly a mark of the Spirit's work in an individual." See *1-2 Timothy & Titus*, page 228.

fear of God in "the most excellent governor Felix" when he spoke to him about "righteousness, *self-control*, and the judgment to come."[77] The verb form of "egkratēs" appears only twice. Paul used the Olympic athlete metaphor for the Christian life in 1 Corinthians 9:25, "And everyone who competes for the prize is *temperate* in all things," "all athletes are *disciplined* in their training (NLT)," or "goes into *strict training* (NIV)." He used it earlier in this letter to speak to single Christians: "If they cannot *exercise self-control*, let them marry. For it is better to marry than to burn with passion (7:9)." Several commentators on the book of Titus say that this Greek word includes controlling your sexual passions and lusts.[78]

"Egkratēs" literally means "en" (in) + "kratos" (power, dominion, strength). It is someone who has "power over," or better, "mastery over" his passions, emotions, and actions. He overcomes. The basic idea of the Greek verb for "kratos" is Romans 6:14, "For sin shall not have *dominion over* you, for you are not under law but under grace" or "for sin shall not be your *master*." Stott defines it as "self-mastery" and Hiebert as "one in control of strength" who "refrains from all that is unlawful and harmful."[79] Interestingly, "akratēs," or those "without self-control," will be one of the defining characteristics of those living in the perilous times of the last days in 2 Timothy 3:3. We all see it today – people are wild and out of control.

While quoting Proverbs 25:28 – "A person without self-control is like a city with broken-down walls (NLT)" – Strauch defines this word for self-control as "an undisciplined man who has little resistance to sexual lust, provocation, anger, slothfulness, a critical spirit, or other desires that seek to control him. He is easy prey to sinful desires and the devil. Self-control is an essential part of the Christian life. Leaders who lack discipline frustrate their fellow leaders as well as those they lead. Not only are they poor examples, but they cannot accomplish what needs to

---

[77] See Acts 24:25.
[78] See, for example, Yarbrough, page 487 or Mounce, page 391.
[79] *The Message of 1 Timothy & Titus*, Stott, page 177 and *Titus and Philemon*, D. Edmond Hiebert, Everyman's Bible Commentary, Mood Press, page 35.

be done. Consequently, the flocks they shepherd are poorly managed and cared for."[80]

We live in an age where so many people are out of control. Every day we hear of people – including Christians – ruining their lives because they didn't exercise self-control. Out of control anger or rage results in murder. People abuse alcohol and drugs. Many have no restraint over their tongue and say hurtful things that they deeply regret later. Men and women wreck their marriages and families through adultery and fornication. Yarbrough says, "It takes twenty years to build a reputation, but only five minutes to destroy it."[81]

As an elder, you're going to deal with many tense people and situations. You need to remain calm. You can't be impulsive. You'll need to pray and have the Holy Spirit restrain you.

Let me give you some practical thoughts about self-control as an overseer or elder.

If someone has angered you or you need to confront people who are on edge, spend a lot of time in prayer before meeting with them.

Years ago, I was very agitated and frustrated with a man in our church. He was so demeaning and prideful toward his wife. He constantly badgered her. He provoked her to anger. His wife had moved out several times but always seemed to go back. Within a few weeks they would again be at each other's throats. *This went on for years.*

I had had enough. I called him and told him that I was coming over to his house. There was an angry tone in my voice. I was going to straighten him out once and for all!

Before I went to his house, I had to stop off at the church to get something. While I was there, I walked into the main sanctuary. I was so upset that I decided at the last minute to just spend a few minutes in prayer. Thank God, I ended up staying for more than one hour. The Lord put it on my heart to pray for this person, bless him, and even *give thanks for him.* My heart was so contrary. I wanted to throw him out of the window! I was hot!

---

[80] *Biblical Eldership*, Strauch, page 179.
[81] *The Letters of Timothy and Titus*, Yarbrough, page 488.

The Holy Spirit really humbled me that day. "Son, you are out of control. Whatever you are getting ready to say is going to cause a lot of damage. Begin to give thanks to God for him." These words changed my bad attitude. It empowered me with the grace of God. I still wasn't practicing that word of wisdom from Proverbs – "A gentle answer turns away wrath, but a harsh word stirs up anger."[82]

Then these verses flooded my mind: "See that no one renders evil for evil to anyone, but always pursue what is good both for yourselves and for all," "do not repay anyone evil for evil. Be careful to do what is right in the eyes of everybody," and "do not repay evil with evil or insult with insult, but with blessing, because to this you were called so that you may inherit a blessing."[83] Interestingly, I was getting ready to act just like him! The old saying is "if you're bit by a snake, don't become one."

You can never overcome evil with evil. Evil is only overcome with good. Once again, when you are angry with someone, spend lots of time in prayer for yourself and others.

Don't let other people's whims and desires dictate the Lord's agenda for the church.

You know what a whim is, right? It's a fleeting thought or fad. It's a sudden thought, idea, or desire, especially one based on impulse rather than reason or necessity. There are so many experts in the church. They know what is best, and certainly, they can run the church better than you. They have great ideas that everyone needs to adopt. More often than not, they are nothing more than complainers who are never content.

I've been given many books on subjects I should be preaching. I've been given many invitations to outreaches our churches should be doing. I've been introduced to many ministers who should be teaching at our church. But just because everyone else is doing it doesn't mean that I/we should be doing it. I tell pastors again and again that they should only do what God has given them grace to do. Paul said, "I am who I am by the grace of

---

[82] See Proverbs 15:1.
[83] See 1 Thessalonians 5:15; Romans 12:17; and 1 Peter 3:9.

God, and it was His grace that was working in me."[84] We will quickly burnout doing what God told everyone else to do!

I'll never forget a man in our church who kept insisting that we needed to have church fellowships and potlucks at local parks. He kept mentioning this "great idea" to me over several months until I finally gave in. As we organized the event, this man did very little to help us, and when we finally went to the park one Saturday afternoon, he didn't even come! The truth is, a few weeks later, he stopped attending our church! Did we enjoy ourselves? Yes. Was it a profitable event? Of course. But it was a lot of work and required a lot of people to help.

Stay focused. Be self-controlled. Be kind and learn to say "NO" to many good ideas.

Another similar area is all the invitations I receive to attend ministry dinners, fundraisers, outreaches, revivals, mission trips, Easter events, Christmas plays, and prayer meetings. So many good people inviting me to worthy causes. They will bombard you with emails, flyers, text messages, and phone calls. I want to help. I want to show my concern and support. I feel guilty when I have to say "no." Again, I need to stay focused and self-controlled with my time and schedule. I could stay busy full-time attending everyone's events!

An elder should never need to curse, threaten, or yell at someone in his flock. You've crossed a line and you're going to hurt people badly.

I remember one time that I had a meeting with the main leaders/elders of our church. During the meeting, one of the elders (an older man) spoke against nearly everything I was bringing up. He came to the meeting with a bad attitude. I became so upset with this man's actions, I finally adjourned the meeting and told this man, "Please stay after the meeting because I want to talk to you."

Thankfully, another leader saw the anger on my countenance and he wrote on a piece of paper, *1 Timothy 5:1 – "Don't speak angrily to an older man. But talk to him like he was your father."* I saw the Lord's intervention in that verse and it calmed me down enough to talk to this elderly man in a civilized

---

[84] See 1 Corinthians 15:10.

manner. I was getting ready to blast him for his comments in that meeting.

I once had to convene a special meeting at the church because one of the men had committed adultery and scandalized many members. I was so upset by what he did. What really infuriated me was that he had been around my daughter in recent weeks. I made the serious mistake of taking my angry spirit to the meeting instead of taking everything to the Lord. I actually used the word, "hell," in one sentence when talking to all the leaders. Again, thankfully, my wife was sitting next to me and she tugged my shirt as if to say, "Stop it! Sit down!" After that, I sat down, stayed quiet for a moment, and then apologized to the group for my words. The elder must be self-controlled.

In Luke 9:54-56, it reads, "When James and John saw this, they said, 'Lord, do You want us to command fire to come down from heaven and consume them, just as Elijah did?' But He turned and rebuked them, and said, 'You do not know what manner of spirit you are of. For the Son of Man did not come to destroy men's lives but to save them.'" This is a great word of self-control for all leaders – Jesus came to save, not destroy. We should never threaten anyone with God's judgment or wrath. You can rebuke a man without threatening him with death and destruction.

In perhaps the most bitter and difficult situation I've ever had to deal with, I made a threat of God's judgment upon a man who rebelled against the Lord, spoke evil of me to many others, and caused significant division and strife in our church. My pastoral supervisor, an elderly and godly man, had to correct me and tell me never to threaten people like that again. I had to humble myself and repent of my words.[85]

These two verses are appropriate: "If it is possible, as much as depends on you, live peaceably with all men. Beloved, do not avenge yourselves, but rather give place to wrath; for it is written, 'Vengeance is Mine, I will repay,' says the Lord" and

---

[85] Sad to say, within a year or two, this man actually died of a drug overdose. He was only in his early fifties.

"For we know Him who said, 'Vengeance is Mine, I will repay,' says the Lord. And again, 'The Lord will judge His people.'"[86]

Exercise self-control. Let God judge His people. May the Holy Spirit restrain us so we can live in self-control.

---

[86] See Romans 12:18-19 and Hebrews 10:30.

9

The Church Leader Must Be Just

*"For a bishop must be hospitable, a lover of what is good, sober-minded, **just**, holy, self-controlled."*
(Titus 1:8)

Harold Franks was killed outside a neighborhood convenience store on May 19, 1975. According to detectives, Franks had acid splashed on his face, was clubbed, and shot several times. The robbers took $425 and fled. A 12-year-old, African-American paperboy, Eddie Vernon, said he knew the men who killed Franks. Vernon identified Ricky Jackson as the man who shot Franks, Ronnie Bridgeman doused him with acid, and Ronnie's brother, Wiley, drove the getaway car. In 1975, all three men were found guilty of the murder and sentenced to die in the electric chair. In 1977, due to a technicality, the sentence was reduced to life in prison without parole.

The only problem was that the police coerced the young Eddie Vernon to lie about what happened. The murder weapon was never found. Jackson and the Bridgeman brothers were not at the scene of the crime. Vernon could not even identify any of the accused men in a police line-up.

When the truth was finally told and Jackson was released from an Ohio prison, he had served 39 years behind bars. According to the Smithsonian Magazine, it was longest prison term for an exonerated defendant in American history. The magazine wrote, "It is a staggering example of how the criminal justice system can wrong the innocent."[87]

All true Christians must actively and openly oppose injustice wherever it is found. As Martin Luther King Jr. famously said, "Injustice anywhere is a threat to justice everywhere."

Paul told Titus that an overseer "must be just." The dictionary defines "just" as "fair and impartial; acting with fairness; valid and reasonable; done, pursued, or given in accordance with what is morally right." John Calvin defined it as someone "who does not harm anyone."[88] Paul instructed "masters" to be "just and fair" when treating their slaves.[89]

The Lord gave David a powerful truth about those who "rule over" others. "He who rules over men must be *just*, ruling in the fear of God."[90] The elder rules over his household and the house of God. He constantly makes decisions and renders judgments that must be fair and reasonable. He must be level-headed and reject personal favoritism. The classic call of Micah 6:8 applies to church leaders: "He has shown you, O man, what is good; and what the Lord requires of you, *to do justly*, to love mercy, and to walk humbly with your God."

A church leader cannot be unjust. Job 34:17 asks the convicting question, "Should one who hates justice govern?" It is by the wisdom of God that "kings reign, and *rulers decree justice*."[91]

Many godly men in the Bible were described as "just": Simeon, "this man was *just* and devout"; Joseph was "a *just* man"; John the Baptist was "a *just* and holy man"; Joseph of Arimathea was "a good and *just* man"; "Noah was a *just* man"; and Cornelius the centurion was "a *just* man."[92] Most importantly, the Lord Jesus Christ is called "the Just One," "the Just Man," "the Just

---

[87] See *Smithsonian Magazine, "An American Incarceration: Special Report"* by Matthew Shaer, January 2017.

[88] *1-2 Timothy & Titus*, Calvin, page 184.

[89] See Colossians 4:1.

[90] See 2 Samuel 23:3.

[91] See Proverbs 8:15.

[92] See Luke 2:25; Matthew 1:19; Mark 6:20; Luke 23:50; Genesis 6:9; Acts 10:22.

Person," or simply "Just."[93] The prophet Zechariah saw a "King coming to you who is *just* and having salvation."[94] Peter described His suffering as "the *just* dying for the unjust."[95]

Isaiah said that God is "a just God"; Paul wrote that "God is just"; Nehemiah said, "You are just"; and David said, "God is a just judge."[96] God's ways, God's law, and God's ordinances are all just for He "loves justice."[97] When we confess our sins, "He is faithful and *just* to forgive us our sins and to cleanse us from all unrighteousness."[98] God really hates injustice because "he who justifies the wicked, and he who condemns the just, both of them alike are an abomination to the Lord."[99]

What are some practical ways that the elder must be fair and just with the local church?

The elder must be just in how he treats the poor, widow, fatherless, and weak. James reminds us all that we are to treat the "poor man" and the "rich man" the same. There can be no personal favoritism. Ezekiel said that "the man who is just" "gives his bread to the hungry and covers the naked with clothing."[100]

The elder must handle the church's finances with complete integrity and righteousness. Isaiah 26:7 says that "the way of the just is uprightness." The elder must never use the church's money for his advantage. He must work with a church board or financial council who will ensure that not one penny of the Lord's money is mishandled. The tithe is holy to God and must be managed in the fear of God. He must ensure that all debts are paid promptly, taxes filed accurately, building permits secured timely, and key staff paid fairly.

The elder is a model of faith and faithfulness in the local congregation. He is a faithful attender, faithful tither, faithful

---

[93] See Acts 7:52, 22:14; Matthew 27:19, 27:24; Acts 3:15.
[94] See Zechariah 9:9.
[95] See 1 Peter 3:18.
[96] See Isaiah 45:21; Romans 3:26; Nehemiah 9:33; Psalm 7:11.
[97] See Revelation 15:3; Romans 7:12; Nehemiah 9:13; Isaiah 61:8; Psalm 37:28.
[98] See 1 John 1:9.
[99] See Proverbs 17:15.
[100] See Ezekiel 18:7.

servant, and faithful prayer warrior in the church. Four times the Bible tells us that "the just shall live by faith." And Hebrews 10:38-39 reads, "Now the just shall live by faith; but if anyone draws back, My soul has no pleasure in him. But we are not of those who draw back to perdition, but of those who believe to the saving of the soul." Elders are not "drawing back;" we are moving forward. We are encouraging the flock by our strong belief in the Lord's miracle-working power. Our faith in the Lord should motivate, strengthen, and edify the believers in our midst.

The issue of justice involves how we treat other people, but holiness involves our direct relationship to the Lord. The elder must be holy. Let's cover that in the next chapter.

10

The Church Leader Must Be Holy

*"A bishop must be hospitable, a lover of what is good, sober-minded, just, **holy**, self-controlled."*
(Titus 1:8)

This requirement seems pretty obvious. The Lord requires all Christians to be holy – "As He who called you is holy, you also be holy in all your conduct, because it is written, 'Be holy, for I am holy.'"[101]

When we think of "holy," many believers remember the main Greek word for "holy," which is "hagios" and its derivatives:

- There's "hagiazō" which means "sanctified; consecrated" as in *"Sanctify* them by Your truth. Your word is truth."
- "Hagiasmos" or "sanctification; holiness" as in "God did not call us to uncleanness, but in *holiness.*"
- "Hagion" or "holy place; sanctuary; holy temple" as in "having boldness to enter the *Holiest* by the blood of Jesus."
- "Hagios" or "Holy Spirit; saints; holy" as in "they do not rest day or night, saying: '*Holy, holy, holy,* Lord God Almighty, Who was and is and is to come."

---

[101] See 1 Peter 1:15-16, quoted from Leviticus 11:44-45, 19:2.

- "Hagiotēs" or "sanctity; a state of holiness" as in "building yourselves up on your *most holy* faith."
- "Hagiōsunē" or "sacredness; holiness" as in "perfecting *holiness* in the fear of God."[102]

These six words appear 275 times in the New Testament, and some form of the words "holy," "sanctify," or "consecrate" appear over 1,000 times in the Bible. Obviously, this is a major theme of the Scriptures.

Interestingly, Paul did not use any of these words here in Titus 1:8. He used the Greek adjective, "hosios,"[103] which Knight defines as "devout, pious, or pleasing to God."[104] Other translations use "pure," "be devoted to God," or "live a devout life." Barclay describes it as "the person who reverences the fundamental decencies of life, the things which go back beyond any human law."[105] This word is used as an attribute of the holiness of Christ, so it has a very high moral quality. In Acts, Jesus is called "the *Holy* One," and as the Great High Priest in Hebrews, He "is *holy*, harmless, undefiled, separate from sinners, and has become higher than the heavens."[106] When "the song of the Lamb" is sung before the seven last plagues are poured out, it includes the line, "Who shall not fear You, O Lord, and glorify Your name? For You alone are *holy*."[107]

Along with all Christians, elders are supposed to "put on the new man which was created according to God, in true righteousness and *holiness* (hosiotēs)." Paul reminded the Thessalonian believers how he and his companions behaved "*devoutly* (hosiōs) and justly and blamelessly among you."[108]

What does it mean that an elder should be holy?

---

[102] See John 17:17; 1 Thessalonians 4:7; Hebrews 10:19; Revelation 4:8; Jude 20; and 2 Corinthians 7:1.

[103] Paul will use the antonym, "anosios," in 1 Timothy 1:9 to say that the law is for the "unholy," and in the perilous times of the last days, we would see "unholy" people in abundance (2 Timothy 3:2).

[104] *The Pastoral Epistles*, Knight, page 292. This is also the definition given by Arndt/Gingrich.

[105] *The Letters of Timothy, Titus, and Philemon*, Barclay, page 269.

[106] See Acts 2:27, 13:35; Hebrews 7:26.

[107] See Revelation 15:4.

[108] See 1 Thessalonians 2:10.

In his best-selling book, *The Pursuit of Holiness*, author Jerry Bridges makes these deep and powerful statements: "As we grow in holiness, we grow in hatred of sin; and God, being infinitely holy, has an infinite hatred of sin. We cannot escape the fact that God hates our sins. We may trifle with our sins or excuse them, but God hates them. Therefore, every time we sin, we are doing something God hates. He hates our lustful thoughts, our pride and jealousy, and our outbursts of temper. We need to be gripped by the fact that God hates all these things. We need to cultivate in our own hearts the same hatred of sin God has. Hatred of sin lies at the root of all true holiness."[109] Let us never forget, as John Calvin wrote long ago, that to be holy always "refers to your relationship to God."[110]

As a holy elder, you must live a holy and sanctified life. You must be devoted to God, your wife and family, and the local church where you serve. You cannot be compromising with sin in any area of your life. You must teach holiness to God's flock on a regular basis. Holiness must be your priority and pursuit – "Pursue holiness, without which no one will see the Lord."[111]

Since I came to our church in 1991, pastors in our city have committed adultery, had sex with teenage girls in the youth group, stolen large amounts of money, divorced their wives, were caught with large amounts of pornography on their computers, preached false doctrines and heresies, and spiritually abused many sincere Christian believers. As James wrote, "My brethren, these things ought not to be so."[112] Any church leader pursuing holiness will flee from these things.

A very important part of an elder's holiness involves his sexuality. When speaking about sexual issues in the church, Paul told Christians, "For this is the will of God, your sanctification: that you should abstain from sexual immorality…for God did not call us to uncleanness, but to holiness." Another translation reads, "God's will is for you to be holy, so stay away from all sexual sin. Then each of you will control his own body and live in holiness

---

[109] *The Pursuit of Holiness*, Jerry Bridges, NavPress, Colorado Springs, Colorado, page 28.
[110] *1 & 2 Timothy & Titus*, Calvin, page 184.
[111] See Hebrews 12:14.
[112] See James 3:10.

and honor."[113] Paul gave Timothy the proper focus: "Treat older women as mothers, and younger women as sisters, with absolute purity."[114] There will be many pretty, young women in the church, but they must be treated with *absolute purity* as if they are your own sisters. We are there to protect them, not use them.

Never meet alone with any woman, especially those in your church or ministry. Never counsel any woman alone. Let the older ladies in your church do that.

Recently, many pastors and elders have gotten into trouble because they've sent completely inappropriate text messages or social media posts to other women. Any comments to women must be kept on a professional level and with "absolute purity." If you are texting with a married woman in your church over church business or legitimate issues, include her husband in the chats. If for some good reason[115] you shouldn't send it to the husband, include your wife.

When women come up for prayer during a service, especially attractive women or single women, make sure your wife is standing next to you. You can also have other designated women come up to pray for these ladies. A lot of unfriendly and ungodly transfer takes place when people come up for the wrong reasons.

Never travel alone or stay in hotel rooms by yourself. Take your wife, children, or another Christian brother. Pay the extra costs and protect yourself. There's a critical reason why Paul always traveled with Barnabas, Silas, Timothy, and others. Jesus sent His disciples "two by two."[116] So many ministers have been tempted and fallen when they've stayed alone in hotels.

Never forget the warning of 1 Peter 5:8-9: "Stay alert! Watch out for your great enemy, the devil. He prowls around like a roaring lion, looking for someone to devour. Stand firm against him, and be strong in your faith. Remember that your Christian brothers and sisters all over the world are going through the same kind of suffering you are."

Be holy, for the Lord is holy.

---

[113] See 1 Thessalonians 4:3-4, 7.
[114] See 1 Timothy 5:2.
[115] For example, if the husband is unsaved.
[116] See Luke 10:1, for example.

11

The Church Leader Must be Gentle

*"Not given to wine, not violent, not greedy for money, **but gentle**, not quarrelsome, not covetous."*
(1 Timothy 3:3)

I need to be honest – I don't know too many pastors who are known for their gentleness. Nevertheless, Paul said that bishops must be "gentle." When you look at 1 Timothy 3:3 carefully, you'll see that "gentle" is the only noun or adjective in this verse that doesn't have the negative Greek particle (adverb), "not," in front of it. All the other five do. The "gentle" leader cannot be "violent" and "quarrelsome." Gentleness "points to a considerate and patient forbearance that would not tolerate any violent methods."[117]

Just today, I went to visit a mother who gave birth to a beautiful boy. The baby was so delicate and tiny. I saw how this mother handled that baby with extreme care. She had the baby wrapped up in a warm blanket. She gently touched his hair and straighten it to expose his forehead. This mother showed nothing but very tender kindness and gentleness to her child.

Amazingly, Paul would describe the life of "apostles of Christ" in these words: "We were *gentle* among you, just as a

---

[117] *The Pastoral Epistles*, Guthrie, page 93.

nursing mother cherishes her own children."[118] Honestly, most Christian men I know – including church leaders – are not kind or gentle. We are rough. We are harsh. We can be mean. Calvin says we should "not be feared on account of our severity."[119] I've met many Christian leaders who are imposing and intimidating. Who will bring their problems to such a leader?

One of the character qualities that first drew my attention to my wife was her gentleness. She was very meek and humble and still is. She worked as a kindergarten teacher for many years and she learned how to treat these little children with gentleness. When Peter described a woman's true outward "adornment," he wrote about "the hidden person of the heart, with the incorruptible beauty of a *gentle* and quiet spirit, which is very precious in the sight of God."[120] This describes my wife.

The men need to learn from the women. Many Christian women are gentle.

All this talk about women, mothers, nursing mothers, and newborn babies can sound pretty mushy and foreign to Christian men. We're into toughness, not gentleness. However, Jesus said, "Take My yoke upon you and learn from Me, for I am *gentle* and lowly in heart, and you will find rest for your souls."[121] Paul spoke of "the meekness and *gentleness* of Christ."[122] No Christian man would ever say that Jesus was weak or feminine. He was the man of all men. He was a man's man. All Christians want to be like Him.

Not only did Paul say that church leaders must be gentle, he also commanded Timothy to seek it in his own life. He writes, "But you, O man of God, flee these things and pursue

---

[118] See 1 Thessalonians 2:7.

[119] *1 & 2 Timothy & Titus*, Calvin, page 56.

[120] See 1 Peter 3:4.

[121] See Matthew 11:29. The Greek word here for "gentle" can also be defined as "meek" or someone who is "mild."

[122] See 2 Corinthians 10:1. Yarbrough explains, "'Gentle' can conjure up the picture of a weak leader who blandly accepts whatever happens with a helpless smile." See *The Letters of Timothy and Titus*, Yarbrough, page 197.

righteousness, godliness, faith, love, patience, and *gentleness*."[123] Paul was commanding him to flee ungodly things and follow after gentleness. When was the last time you "pursued gentleness?"

Paul lists "gentleness" as one of the fruit of the Spirit: "But the fruit of the Spirit is love, joy, peace, longsuffering, kindness, goodness, faithfulness, *gentleness*, and self-control. Against such there is no law."[124] Without a doubt, only the Holy Spirit can produce this character quality in the life of a believer. It is not natural for a man to be gentle.

I looked up the word, "gentle," in the dictionary. It is defined as "not severe, rough, or violent; mild; kind; amiable." The Greek word often translated as "gentleness" is defined as "mild." It is a mild-mannered person. One commentator defines the word as "sweet reasonableness."[125]

I love how Paul calls all Christians to a life of gentleness. It is a character quality all of us should cultivate by the Spirit's power. He would write, "I beseech you to walk worthy of the calling with which you were called, with all lowliness and *gentleness*, with longsuffering, bearing with one another in love" and "to speak evil of no one, to be peaceable, *gentle*, showing all humility to all men."[126] James asserts that "the wisdom that is from above is first pure, then peaceable, *gentle*, willing to yield, full of mercy and good fruits, without partiality and without hypocrisy."[127] There is something peaceful about gentleness. It is willing to yield. It is full of mercy and good fruits. There is a "lowliness" and "humility" about it that every Christian needs.

It's pretty obvious that *all* Christians need gentleness. This is the Christ-like nature that every believer must exhibit. Christ was gentle; so must His followers be. If every Christian must be gentle, then certainly every Christian leader must also be gentle. The leader must provide the example.

---

[123] See 1 Timothy 6:11. Paul uses two imperative present tense Greek verbs to command Timothy to continuous action in this pursuit. He was to flee from certain things and pursue others.

[124] See Galatians 5:22-23.

[125] *First Timothy*, Hiebert, page 66. The quote is attributed to Matthew Arnold.

[126] See Ephesians 4:1-2 and Titus 3:2.

[127] See James 3:17.

But why is "gentleness" so important to bishops and elders? What does this mean practically?

Paul told Timothy and Titus – the very men who were instructed on the main qualifications of church elders – "to rebuke with all authority" and to use Scripture for "rebuking, correcting, and training."[128] If you've been a church leader for any length of time, you know you'll have to warn, rebuke, and correct people regularly. This is never a pleasant task, but nevertheless, it is very necessary and biblical.

Christians in church are going to do things that will make you angry. You're going to be tested again and again. They will try your patience. They will say unkind things about you and others. They will do ungodly things that will make you want to pull out your hair (literally Nehemiah did this!). You're going to have to keep your temper in check. As we've already written, you must exercise self-control. The next four chapters of this book will teach us that church leaders cannot be "quarrelsome," "violent," "soon angry," or "self-willed." It is during these times that you might be tempted to "strike the rock twice" and yell, "You rebels" like Moses did. Don't do this. Exercise gentleness.

Here's what we're told to do: "Brethren, if a man is overtaken in any trespass, you who are spiritual restore such a one in *a spirit of gentleness*, considering yourself lest you also be tempted." "A servant of the Lord must not quarrel but *be gentle to all*, able to teach, patient, in humility correcting those who are in opposition, if God perhaps will grant them repentance, so that they may know the truth." "What do you want? Shall I come to you with a rod, or in love and *a spirit of gentleness*?"[129]

I remember a few years ago, three men in our church were given tickets for driving under the influence (DUI). Three men who name the name of Christ were drunk while driving. Three! All in one year! I couldn't believe it. It made me angry. What were they thinking?

Over the years, Christian men have confessed to me that they have had adulterous affairs, gotten drunk, viewed pornography, visited a prostitute in another city, physically beaten

---

[128] See Titus 3:2 and 2 Timothy 3:16.
[129] See Galatians 6:1; 2 Timothy 2:24-25; 1 Corinthians 4:21.

their wives, threatened to kill someone, had sexual intercourse with their girlfriend, gotten a girl pregnant, stolen property from work, cheated on their taxes, lied to their employers, deceived their wives, and believed false doctrine and heresies. One man was a peeping Tom who had physically exposed himself to a neighbor's wife. I'm sorry this is so crude and unholy, but this happens in a local church. I've heard many stories from many different pastors of the incredibly foolish things that Christians have done to ruin their lives!

Should this really surprise us? Jesus rebuked the churches in Revelation for sexual immorality, spiritual deadness, lukewarm Christianity, cold love, and believing false teachings. He commanded them to repent. Paul severely chastised the Corinthians for offering sacrifices to idols, committing fornication, getting drunk at the communion table, misusing spiritual gifts, believing heretical doctrine, taking other Christians to court before unbelievers, and divorcing and defrauding their spouses. What a mess! It's incredible that Paul still saw them as a church, and they were the proof of his apostleship in the Lord! Talk about grace!

My point is this: You are going to deal with many people and many situations that are very difficult. You will have to confront many corrupt and shameful things in the lives of God's people. You will have to restore people. You need to speak the truth in love. Paul said "those who are spiritual must restore people in a spirit of gentleness." When people oppose you, you cannot be quarrelsome, "but be gentle to all, patient, in humility correcting those who are in opposition." God is the One who must grant them repentance.

Strauch strikes the right tone: "A gentle man exhibits a willingness to yield and patiently makes allowances for the weakness and ignorance of the fallen human condition. He is gracious, reasonable, and considerate. One who is gentle refuses to retaliate in kind for wrong done by others, and does not insist upon the letter of the law or personal rights. He possesses God's pure, peaceable, gentle, reasonable, and merciful wisdom."[130]

---

[130] *Biblical Eldership*, Strauch, pages 199-200.

I remember a pastor friend who came to talk to me about a situation that was threatening to tear his church apart. He was having a very hard time with his worship leader and others on the worship team. They were not being submissive to the desires and wishes of this pastor. The stress and tension were beginning to take its toll on the pastor and the congregation. The conflicts were beginning to spill over onto others. A "root of bitterness had sprung up causing trouble, and by this many others were becoming defiled."[131] He asked me what he should do.

After some discussion back and forth, I quoted Paul's word to the Corinthians – "What do you want? Shall I come to you with a rod, or in love and a spirit of gentleness?"[132] I told this pastor to offer the worship leader and others two options – do you want the pastor to deal with you with a rod or do you want him to do things in love and a spirit of gentleness? Unfortunately, the people didn't want to change and the pastor had to use the rod. The worship leader quit and others left with him. To the praise of God, the church got back on track and the congregation experienced new growth and peace.

I use this example because sometimes gentleness doesn't work with people. However, it is something you always want to do first. Always approach people with gentleness. Don't be heavy-handed. Use your authority to build others up, not tear them down.[133]

Let me offer this advice – if you must go to any meeting with your church members where you're going to correct and rebuke them, please do it in a "spirit of gentleness." If you are harsh and heavy-handed, you could cause a lot of damage. Before you go, pray, give thanks to God for them, and ask God for wisdom and the right words. I love that word in Proverbs that says "the preparations of the heart belong to man, but the answer of the tongue is from the Lord" (16:1). The Lord will give you just the right words. Christian leader, "Let your gentleness be known to all men."

---

[131] See Hebrews 12:15.
[132] See 1 Corinthians 4:21.
[133] See 2 Corinthians 10:8 and 13:10.

In the next chapter, we begin a series of eight "must nots." There are character qualities that must not be in church leaders. Some appear obvious. Let's start with the first one – the church leader must not be quarrelsome.

8 Qualifications the Church Leader Must Not Be

- He must NOT be Quarrelsome

- He must NOT be Violent

- He must NOT be Soon Angry

- He must NOT be Self-Willed

- He must NOT be Greedy for Money

- He must NOT be Covetous

- He must NOT be Given to Wine

- He must NOT be a Novice

12

The Church Leader Must Not Be Quarrelsome

*"Not given to wine, not violent, not greedy for money, but gentle, **not quarrelsome**, not covetous."*
(1 Timothy 3:3)

This chapter and the next seven chapters involve things that must NOT be in the elder's life – NOT quarrelsome, NOT violent, NOT soon angry, NOT self-willed, NOT greedy for money, NOT covetous, NOT given to wine, and NOT a novice. Very often, when you want to learn about something, one of the best ways to define it is by what it's not. For example, when Paul wanted to describe true agape love in 1 Corinthians 13, he listed everything it was not: "Love does *not* envy; love does *not* parade itself, is *not* puffed up; does *not* behave rudely, does *not* seek its own, is *not* provoked, does *not* keep a record of wrongs; and does *not* rejoice in iniquity." You can know what love truly is by looking at what it is not. This is true of biblical eldership. It's very important to look carefully at all the "nots."

Paul writes that the bishop "must not be quarrelsome." The KJV translated it as "not a brawler." Most modern translations give it a positive twist – "peaceful," "peaceable," "peace-loving," "kind," or "forbearing." This Greek word's only other occurrence is in Titus 3:2, "...to speak evil of no one, *to be peaceable*, gentle, showing all humility to all men." The word is "amachos," which is the negative particle "a = un," + "machos = strife, fight, contention." It basically means "to abstain from fighting; not contentious." I think the best word is the NAS translation, "uncontentious." Barclay defines it as "disinclined to fight…and real Christian leaders want nothing so much as they want peace with other people."[134]

An elder must be free of relationship arguments and conflicts. If a person "delights in airing his own opinions" (Proverbs 18:2), he will not make a good elder. This requirement goes along with "he must not be violent." When Paul listed the works of the flesh in Galatians 5, four of them were "contentions, outbursts of wrath, dissensions, and factions." You need men of the Spirit, not of the flesh.

Before I knew the Lord, when I was a teenager in high school, I was a brawler. I was very angry. I provoked others. I started fights. If someone looked at me the wrong way, I would start swinging. I remember going to a party my senior year in high school in a very isolated location. I went to the party looking for a fight. One man at the party stared at me for a few moments and I went over and punched him in the mouth. We rolled around on the ground before several people broke up the fight. I was quarrelsome.

Thank God for Jesus Christ and His salvation and grace. While I did struggle with anger for many years, I no longer felt the need to start a brawl.

A church leader needs to be calm, gentle, and self-controlled. You will face many tense situations. I officiated a funeral once where the family of the ex-wife started a fight with the current wife right in front of the casket of the deceased husband. For many days afterward, the ex-wife tried to drag me into her jealous rage. Proverbs 26:17 reads, "He who passes by and meddles in a quarrel not his own is like one who takes a dog by the ears." If you grab a dog by the ears, you will get bit! I refused to have anything to do with old fights and strife.

Christians like to argue about doctrine, politics, and ex-husbands. 2 Timothy 2:23-24 says, "Don't have anything to do with foolish and stupid arguments, because you know they

---

[134] *The Letters to Timothy, Titus, and Philemon*, Barclay, page 94.

produce quarrels. And the Lord's servant must not quarrel." In Titus 3:9-10, it reads, "But avoid foolish controversies and genealogies and arguments and quarrels about the law, because these are unprofitable and useless. Warn a divisive person once, and then warn him a second time. After that, have nothing to do with him." James said, "What causes fights and quarrels among you? Don't they come from your desires that battle within you? You want something but don't get it. You kill and covet, but you cannot have what you want. You quarrel and fight."

This instruction is given to Christians. There always seems to be arguments, quarrels, and fights among God's people. The disciples of Jesus argued and fought over who was the greatest among them.[135] Paul and Barnabas got into such a bad disagreement that they parted ways and never worked together again.[136]

Many years ago, as a young pastor, I appointed a man in our church as an elder. He seemed to be very zealous for the things of God. He was our worship leader. I learned later that this was a serious mistake. He had a nasty temper and he liked to win arguments. He felt like he could order people around who were on the worship team. One time he angrily corrected someone's wife over the phone and this really upset the husband. The husband stopped coming to church. Before you know it, there seemed to be fires all around this man. He got into arguments with many. Soon, he was arguing and fighting with me. He was a quarrelsome elder. He was disqualified from serving. He handled every problem with fights. Even removing him from the elder position was extremely difficult. Don't appoint quarrelsome people!

After suffering with this elder for many months, I learned the truth that one commentator mentions about quarrelsome people – "The overseer must not be quarrelsome. This tendency betrays an inability to get along with and accept the views of others, and perhaps deeper personality flaws as well."[137] Christians who like to argue and fight with others have very deep

---

[135] See Mark 9:34; Luke 9:46; and Luke 22:24.
[136] See Acts 15:36-41.
[137] *1-2 Timothy & Titus*, Towner, page 87.

flaws that are almost impossible to heal. Churches that appoint such people as elders will experience many, many troubles. Never appoint an elder who is aggressive.

There is a word in the Bible that is often associated with angry, quarrelsome people. That word is "strife." It is of Germanic origin (strītan). It means "to quarrel" in German.

The one book of the Bible that gives us the most instruction on "strife" is the book of Proverbs. Notice how it is used: "Hatred stirs up strife," "by pride comes nothing but strife," "a wrathful man stirs up strife," "a perverse man sows strife," "he who loves transgression loves strife," "cast out the scoffer, and contention will leave; yes, strife and reproach will cease," "where there is no talebearer, strife ceases," "as charcoal is to burning coals, and wood to fire, so is a contentious man to kindle strife," "he who is of a proud heart stirs up strife," "an angry man stirs up strife," and "for as churning the milk produces butter, and as twisting the nose produces blood, so stirring up anger produces strife."[138]

According to Proverbs, quarrelsome people are those who are angry, contentious, proud, and gossips. When you remove them from the scene, the fires stop and the arguments end. Peace returns. People begin to work together again. Paul wrote in 1 Timothy 6:4, "He is proud, knowing nothing, but is obsessed with disputes and arguments over words, from which come envy, strife, reviling, and evil suspicions." No church leader is qualified to lead who is quarrelsome. As Kelly writes, "Far from exhibiting 'quarrelsomeness,' he should radiate a spirit of peace and mutual charity in the congregation."[139]

---

[138] See Proverbs 10:12, 13:10, 15:18, 16:28, 17:19, 22:10, 26:20, 26:21, 28:25, 29:22, and 30:33.
[139] *A Commentary on the Pastoral Epistles*, Kelly, page 77.

13

The Church Leader Must Not Be Violent

*"Not given to wine, **not violent**, not greedy for money, but gentle, not quarrelsome, not covetous."*
(1 Timothy 3:3)

*"For a bishop must be blameless, as a steward of God, not self-willed, not quick-tempered, not given to wine, **not violent**, not greedy for money."*
(Titus 1:7)

Many churches and para-church ministries are ministering to men and women coming out of very dark lifestyles. We can all praise the Lord for the powerful conversions and deliverances we are seeing in our midst. People who have had lifelong addictions and bondages are being set free by Christ and the power of the gospel. We have believers in our church presently who have come out of prison, sexual perversion, and terrible dependence on alcohol and drugs.

Because of these evil backgrounds, we must heed the caution of Jude 23: "Rescue those who are living in danger of hell's fire. There are others you should treat with mercy, but be very careful that their filthy lives don't rub off on you." One commentator explains the meaning: "It is a dangerous thing to live for Christ in an atmosphere of false teaching and seductive morals. It is a hazardous thing to try to rescue men for the gospel out of such an environment. If you get too near the fire, it will burn you; if you get too near the garment stained by the flesh, it will defile you."[140] Barclay's warning is necessary: "There is danger to the sinner; but there is also danger to the rescuer. He who would cure an infectious disease runs the risk of infection. The simple fact is that the rescue of those in error is not for everyone to attempt."[141]

There is the ever-present danger of getting burned or getting defiled. In today's culture, there is so much contamination and defilement, it is nearly impossible to avoid getting stained or burned.

There is also the danger of getting angry and violent.

Many years ago, a man came to our church who had perhaps the worst upbringing of any person I had ever encountered. His father abused him physically, mentally, and spiritually in very profound ways. I was amazed that he was still alive.

It shouldn't surprise us that this abused son grew up to be a violent man. As a young teenager, he was already in jail and juvenile hall. A few years later, he was sentenced to ten years in a very notorious prison. He was heavily tattooed and filled with anger and hate. He had a menacing look. He instilled fear and intimidation in others.

By the grace and mercy of God, he was supernaturally converted in prison. When he got out, he continued to serve Christ. He ended up marrying a woman who also had a difficult background who had several children. Soon, they had two more children together – a beautiful little girl and a handsome boy. They attended our church faithfully and were involved in outreach ministries.

One day, everything changed. He began working construction jobs. While at one job site, someone threw a bag of methamphetamines on the floor of the room where he was working. This drug dealer then walked away. All alone and lonely, this father of two precious children took one hit of that

---

[140] *2 Peter & Jude*, Michael Green, Tyndale Commentary Series, Eerdmans Publishing, Grand Rapids, Michigan, page 205.
[141] *The Letters of John and Jude*, William Barclay, The Daily Study Bible Series, Westminster Press, Philadelphia, Pennsylvania, page 205.

drug and it sent him into a terrible time of backsliding that lasted a few years.

I tried to go rescue him. I was so upset that he would do this to himself, his family, and our church family. I was determined to bring him out of darkness, even by force if necessary.

I asked our associate pastor to accompany me. The man's wife told us where we could find him. We went to the house where he was working his construction projects. When he saw me and the associate pastor, he ran out of the back of the house and into a back alley. We both followed in hot pursuit. Somehow, he escaped and we had no idea where he went. We knew he had to come back because he left his vehicle parked on the street in front of the house.

We went back to the house that he left open and we found that the room where he was working was filled with pornographic magazines and videos. He was watching porn on a small TV that he brought to this house. We took all the porn and destroyed it. We disposed of everything in a large trash bin in the alley.

Suddenly, I saw him getting into his large SUV. We ran out of the house and toward the SUV. I yelled at him to stop and talk to us. He started his vehicle and locked the doors. He refused to lower his windows. He turned on his windshield wipers to clean off the morning rain drops.

I hate to admit this to you, but I was so upset that he would not cooperate with us, that in a moment of anger, I jumped onto the hood of his SUV and grabbed the wiper blades. I was kneeling on the hood right in front of him and staring into his eyes.

I was yelling at him to turn off the SUV and get out of it.

Without warning, he put his vehicle into gear and floored it. I fell forward into the windshield. I thought I was going to smash through the window.

His wife had come to the house and saw that I was on top of the vehicle yelling at her husband. She started yelling at me to get off the vehicle or I might get killed.

He kept hitting the gas pedal and the brake over and over again to keep me off balance and hopefully cause me to fall off of the hood. As he finally accelerated down the street, I jumped off the SUV and landed in the middle of the road.

I was so mad at what he did, I was ready to punch him in the face! As I stood there to reflect on what had just happened, I was also mad at myself for doing something so stupid. I could have been run over and killed. It certainly was not worth risking my life in such a situation. His wife was right when she told me that I was crazy. Foolishly, I had allowed my anger, pride, and even violence to get to me. I'll never do that again.[142]

Let us heed Jude's warning and not allow the evil and wickedness of others to defile our spirit. This, of course, was an extreme situation, but elders will face very difficult circumstances. We cannot be given to anger or violence.

The words, "not violent," (mē plēktēs) appear only in 1 Timothy 3:3 and Titus 1:7 as a qualification for bishops and elders. The KJV uses "no striker," and other translations say "not troublemakers" and "he must not like to fight." The Greek word here means someone who will not "flatten out" an opponent. Hiebert translates it, "not quick with his fists," Kelly, "not a giver of blows," and Barclay, "not a man who assaults others."[143] He cannot be "a bully with the tongue or the hand."[144] The plēktēs was a "brawler," "bully," "smiter," or "pugnacious man" according to different Greek dictionaries. "Pugnacious" comes from the Latin word, "pugnus," which means "fist," and defined as "inclined to fight or be aggressive." Thayer's Greek Dictionary defines it as "someone who is contentious and quarrelsome, and quick to come to blows."

Again, elders will face angry, difficult, and tense people, and he must be able to quiet down situations that are ready to explode. He must exercise self-control and restrain his tongue and his actions. He cannot be rash nor provoke people to anger.

In the 4th Century, one of the regulations for ministers in the *Apostolic Constitutions* read, "A bishop, priest or deacon who

---

[142] On a positive note, this man did return to the Lord. Several years later, he came back to our church to apologize to me and others. He is serving the Lord and preaching the gospel to many. God is good.

[143] *Titus and Philemon*, Hiebert, page 33. *A Commentary on the Pastoral Epistles*, Kelly, page 77.

[144] *The Message of 1 Timothy & Titus*, Stott, page 97, quoting Johann Bengel, page 258.

smites the faithful when they err, or the unbelievers when they commit injury, and desires by such means as this to terrify them, we command to be deposed; for nowhere hath the Lord taught us this. When He was reviled, He reviled not again, but the contrary. When He was smitten, He smote not again; when He suffered, He threatened not."[145]

The early church father, Chrysostom, gives us the right perspective: "The teacher is the physician of souls. But the physician does not strike. Rather he heals and restores any who might strike him."[146]

When I first read this requirement for an elder to "not be violent," I thought it was so obvious, that Paul should not have listed it in the first place. However, he was so sure of this that he included it in both lists in Titus and 1 Timothy. I thought I could never turn to violence. "Let him who thinks he stands take heed lest he fall."[147]

Think of Nehemiah. The Bible portrays him as a very godly man. He was certainly a man of prayer and one "who feared God."

Yet, we see him get very upset at his fellow Jews in Nehemiah 13:25: "I rebuked them and called curses down on them. I beat some of the men and pulled out their hair. I made them take an oath in God's name and said: 'You are not to give your daughters in marriage to their sons, nor are you to take their daughters in marriage for your sons or for yourselves.'"

What could cause a man of God like Nehemiah to react so violently? To call down curses, beat them, and pull out their hair sounds fanatical. I don't think most of us know what we're capable of until we get put in that position.

Let us be elders not given to violence. This is something that only evil or wicked men should do.

---

[145] *Apostolic Constitutions*, Section VIII, paragraph 47, page 27.
[146] *Ancient Christian Commentary on Scripture*, Volume IX, page 287.
[147] See 1 Corinthians 10:12.

14

The Church Leader Must Not Be Soon Angry

*"For a bishop must be blameless, as the steward of God; not self-willed, **not soon angry**, not given to wine, no striker, not given to filthy lucre."*
(Titus 1:7)

Moses was very angry.[148] Many things quickly provoked him. In fact, the Bible mentions his anger more than any other person. He was angry with Pharaoh. He was angry with his brother Aaron. He was angry with Eleazar and Ithamar. He was angry at the Israelites. He was angry with his cousin Korah. He was angry with the officers and captains of the army. He was so angry with an Egyptian, that he murdered him and buried him in the sand. At the end of his life, he became enraged at the Israelites, struck the rock twice, and it cost him the Promised Land.

One commentator said this about anger: "The more power a man wields, the more destructive his anger can be."[149] This was true in the life of Moses. More often than not, that anger will not

---

[148] See my book available on Amazon, *The Christian and Anger*, for an extensive treatment on the subject of anger. The first two paragraphs of this chapter were taken from this book (pages 15 and 19).

[149] *Proverbs*, Kenneth T. Aitken, The Daily Study Bible Series, The Westminster Press, Philadelphia, page 108.

come to the surface until it gets under pressure or the fire of difficult situations. Moses was constantly put under very trying circumstances that brought his anger in full view of everyone.

New Testament elders also will face many difficult, stressful, and tense situations in the church body. Christians can get under your skin with their political views, doctrinal beliefs, and marital strife. The church leader must be calm, patient, and understanding. The wisdom of God reminds us that "a quick-tempered man does foolish things" and "a quick-tempered man displays folly."[150] The Bible repeatedly exhorts us to be "slow to anger." We should always thank the Lord that He is "slow to anger" with us!

The Greek adjective that Paul used in Titus 1:7 appears only here in the New Testament. "Mē orgilon" means someone who is "not easily enraged" or "not incited to violent passion." It is a person "not prone to anger." Most modern versions translate it as "not quick-tempered" or "must not be someone who gets angry quickly." One paraphrase uses "impatient." Guthrie says, "…not hot-headed."[151] Barclay calls it an "ingrained anger; not one of the sudden blaze, but the wrath which is continually fed to keep it alive."[152] The verb form, "orgizō," appears eight times including the well-known, "Whoever is *angry* with his brother without a cause shall be in danger of the judgment" from Jesus and "'*Be angry*, and do not sin': do not let the sun go down on your wrath" from Paul.[153] The noun form (orgē) is found thirty-six times and usually translated "wrath," "indignation" or "vengeance."

Let me share with pastors and elders a few thoughts on this subject of "not being soon angry."

When people leave the church. One of the most difficult times in the life of a pastor is when members leave. When they leave, quite often, it is not on good terms.

I remember a new family that came to our church. They had a beautiful family with four children. Both the mother and

---

[150] See Proverbs 14:17 and 14:29.
[151] *The Pastoral Epistles*, Guthrie, page 198.
[152] *The Letters of Timothy, Titus, and Philemon*, Barclay, page 266. He translates it as "he must not be an angry man."
[153] See Matthew 5:22 and Ephesians 4:26.

father had good jobs and they seemed to be a decent, family-oriented household.

Within the first few weeks that they came, someone in our church called out the husband and said publicly, "I believe the Lord has a word for you." She called the person to the front of the church and then spoke a very negative, harsh word over this man. I cringed. The man never came back. Within a few weeks, the family left. They did not return calls. I got very mad because I saw how this man and his family had been unnecessarily offended.

After this incident, I had to instruct our leaders to be careful with "words from the Lord," especially for visitors, and particularly if they are negative or come across as condemning people. In 1 Corinthians 14:3, Paul clearly taught us that "everyone who prophesies speaks to men for their strengthening, encouragement and comfort." Prophecies were meant to bring strength and peace, not insults and offenses.

Many years ago, by God's grace, I helped a man and his wife restore their marriage. The Lord did such a marvelous work in their hearts that they started a marriage cell group in their house. With the agreement of the church leadership, we decided to put the husband through an extensive course of training in counseling and family relationships. We invested a lot of time and money into this couple over the next five years. I appointed him as a lay leader and counselor in our church after he completed all his course work and study. Then, suddenly, they left for another church. He was offered a position as a counselor at a much larger church and it included a salary. Within a few years, he was hired as a police chaplain and counselor.

After all that time and training, they left. I was mad. When they got up in front of the church to announce that they were leaving, it upset many people in the church. Some people felt like they took advantage of us; others felt used.

The chief police chaplain knew me, and he called me because this counselor had applied as a police chaplain. This head chaplain left a voicemail message: "Pastor Charlie, if you recommend him, we will hire him on the spot. We trust your recommendation." For just a flash, I felt I had his career and future in my hands. What was I to do? Years later, I still felt the sting of bad feelings for how he treated me and our church.

Before I called back, I prayed. The Lord melted me with these words: "Bless those who curse you, do good to those who hate you, and pray for those who spitefully use you." I also remembered that verse in Proverbs 19:11, "The discretion of a man makes him slow to anger; it is to his glory to overlook an offense." I also recalled Paul's words in Romans – "Bless and do not curse. Repay no one evil for evil. Do not be overcome by evil, but overcome evil with good."[154]

I gave him the thumbs up. I recommended him for the chaplaincy. He got the job the same day.

Dear fellow elder, God's people don't belong to you; they belong to God. They are not your possession. We must look at the larger kingdom of God. Perhaps it was God's will for this man to be trained at our church and then be sent out to minister to the larger body of Christ and community. Maybe we were just part of the process to get him to where he needed to be. If we are doing it all for the Lord, then He alone should receive all the glory.

Many, many times, I have helped individuals and families by investing countless hours into their lives. Some of them have taken advantage of my help and time. But we must be quick to forgive and continue to serve the Lord with gladness of heart. As Jesus said in the parable of Luke 17, "And does the master thank the servant for doing what he was told to do? Of course not. In the same way, when you obey Me you should say, 'We are unworthy servants who have simply done our duty.'" Our duty is to bless people and strengthen them. Let's leave them where they end up in the hands of the Lord.

When people repeatedly come late to church services or miss them altogether (Dealing with unfaithful and unreliable people). I don't mind telling you – I don't like missing church services. Whenever God's people gather together, I want to be present. I usually arrive at our church facilities on Sunday mornings around 4:30-5:00am. Even when I'm out of town on vacation, my wife and I always try to find a Bible-believing church and attend the Sunday service. I love getting together with the Lord's church to worship, pray, give, and hear the Word of God. Sunday is the Lord's Day, not my day to do whatever I want.

---

[154] See Romans 12:14, 12:17, and 12:21.

Every church has those people who come late to the services. Many times, they disrupt people while trying to find a seat. After the COVID pandemic, so many joined the "pajama church" – they stay in the convenience of their own home and don't fellowship with the rest of the church body. They prefer to see everything on-line at an hour convenient for them. So many of them come to church one Sunday, then you don't see them again for three weeks. Many times, I have crafted my sermons just to reach them in their unfaithfulness, but they don't even show up! I get frustrated and even angry with their lackadaisical attitude toward the things of God.

One of the most difficult truths I've had to deal with is found in James 1:20 – "Man's anger does not bring about the righteous life that God desires." *Anger never works*. It never changes anyone for the good. No amount of anger or yelling is going to make people be more faithful. "Faithfulness" is a fruit of the Spirit in Galatians 5:22, so it cannot be produced by human effort. And about those sermons that I write to target these unreliable people – *Don't come up with sermons for those who are not there but for those who are!* Preach to those who are there every week.

For those people who are inconsistent in their attendance, rather than wait for them to come to you (or the services), you go to them. Meet with them in their house. Go to where they live. They need that personal touch that only the shepherd can give them. When a shepherd has a hundred sheep, he leaves the ninety-nine and goes after the one who goes astray or is lost.

Finally, *anger towards another person in church leadership*. Nearly all church splits have been caused by anger. Paul and Barnabas split up after an angry disagreement. The ten apostles were indignant when James and John wanted to sit on the Lord's right hand and left hand in His glory. Many of God's choice servants have been angry with other leaders.

You will have to deal with pride, jealousy, envy, and selfish ambition in other leaders (and yourself). There will be personality conflicts. You may even disagree over something completely irrelevant to the cause of Christ. All of us have seen angry exchanges and even threats coming from those who "name the name of Christ." I wish all of us were humble, gentle, kind, loving, and willing to yield. The real church world is not that way, even among our best leaders.

This is hard to do and very few of us even consider it, but I think it is vital to maintaining peaceful relationships among church leadership – *Make it your aim to never speak evil of anyone at your church, but especially the pastor and others in leadership.* Paul told the Ephesians, "Let all bitterness, wrath, anger, clamor, and evil speaking be put away from you, with all malice." Peter said, "Lay aside all malice, all deceit, hypocrisy, envy, and all evil speaking." Paul reminded Titus to teach Christians "to speak evil of no one, to be peaceable, gentle, showing all humility to all men."[155] Speak evil of NO ONE. Gossip separates best of friends. When you speak evil of other leaders, anger will rise in your heart against them. You will be "soon angry." You will have a negative attitude against others for whom Christ died. 1 Peter 3:10 reads, "Whoever would love life and see good days must keep his tongue from evil and his lips from deceitful speech."

The elder must not be soon angry.

---

[155] See Ephesians 4:31; 1 Peter 2:1; Titus 3:2.

15

The Church Leader Must Not
Be Self-Willed

*"For a bishop must be blameless, as a steward of
God, **not self-willed**, not quick-tempered, not given to
wine, not violent, not greedy for money."
(Titus 1:7)*

Ll the requirements for elders are important, but I
would have to list this one near the top. A self-
willed elder will introduce regular arguments and
discord at elder meetings. I promise you – your meetings will be
tense and you will have no peace. If you ordain a self-willed
person, you will regret it for years to come.

This requirement is found in Titus 1:7. It's a Greek word
(authadēs) that literally means "autos = self + hēdonē = pleasure,"
or self-pleasing. "Hēdonē" is where we get our English word for
"hedonism" or "the pursuit and devotion to pleasure." The bottom
line – *he is preoccupied with himself.* He is self-willed. Other
translations use the words, "overbearing," "arrogant,"[156] "bossy,"
and "selfish." Fee writes, "God's household manager must be a

---

[156] Mounce uses Proverbs 21:24 as a defining verse for "authadēs" – "A
proud and haughty man — 'Scoffer' is his name; he acts with arrogant
pride." See *Pastoral Epistles*, Mounce, page 390.

servant, not stubbornly self-willed, since it is God's household, not his own."[157]

I like the definition given to this word by Barclay: "The person who is *authadēs* has been described as someone who is so pleased with himself that nothing else pleases him and he is not interested in pleasing anybody."[158]

It is very insightful to see that the only other appearance of this Greek word is in 2 Peter 2:10 to describe false teachers, and it is listed next to words like "presumptuous," "despise authority," "arrogant," and "men who are not afraid to slander celestial beings!" One translation uses the word, "willful." Paul Cedar gives a good definition of this word: "A basic problem of sin is the resistance to submit to God or anyone else. Instead, they prefer to establish themselves as the final authority. They always want their own way."[159] Don't appoint a strong-willed person who always believes his way is the only way.

Is this potential elder submitted to the pastor of the church? Is he always questioning the views or decisions of the pastor and current elders? Is he easily irritated when someone disagrees with him? Is he someone who is unwilling to yield? Is he an easy-going person that works well with others? *A very big test would be how well this man responds to correction. Does he throw things back at you and question why you would dare bring up some issue in his life?* If you must pray days and weeks before you speak a corrective word to this man for fear of rejection or argument, he will definitely not make a good elder. I warn every person responsible for selecting elders, don't ignore this character trait. "Tendencies toward overbearing behavior and anger are indications of unfitness for working as part of a team. Such people do not listen to the views of others but rather force their wills on them, causing disunity."[160]

An elder who is not self-willed flows well with the pastor and the vision of the church. He is easy to deal with and not controlled by self-interests. He will not be overbearing. A good

---

[157] *1 and 2 Timothy*, Fee, page 174.
[158] *The Letters of Timothy, Titus, and Philemon*, Barclay, page 265.
[159] *James, 1, 2 Peter, Jude*, Paul A. Cedar, The Communicator's Commentary, Word Books Publisher, Waco, Texas, page 222.
[160] *1-2 Timothy & Titus*, Towner, page 226.

elder is one who is peaceful and gentle with his wife. Another great test would be to ask his wife if he is self-willed.

Stott says that self-willed leaders "tend to lord it over other people, and to become headstrong and autocratic."[161] The apostle said of elders in 1 Peter 5:3, "Don't lord it over the people assigned to your care, but lead them by your own good example."

Years ago, I appointed a man to not only be our worship leader but also an elder. He was very faithful, hard-working, and zealous for the things of God. He gave generously to the church and was a no-nonsense type of person. He was very supportive of me as the pastor.

Well, through the school of hard knocks, I learned that time-honored truth from President Abraham Lincoln – "Nearly all men can stand adversity, but if you want to test a man's character, give him power." Shortly after appointing him to these positions, he became bossy and overbearing. There was division in the worship team. He believed everyone had to obey his demands. I knew something was wrong when I tried to assign a new believer to him for mentoring and discipleship. This believer told me, "Pastor Charlie, I'll work with any man in the church except him. I have no respect for that man."

When I tried to correct this elder, he became angry. He angered other people in the church. One of the husbands of our singers left the church because of the way he was talking to his wife.

To make a long story short, this man nearly destroyed our church. He caused divisions. He took half the worship team with him to another church. He bad-mouthed me to other pastors in this city. It was one of the ugliest experiences I endured as a local church pastor. This is why I started this chapter speaking of the critical importance of this spiritual requirement. Yarbrough is surely correct when he says, "Paul lists a series of disqualifiers. In popular language, these are no-brainers, immediate warning flags for Titus as prospective pastoral workers come into view." A self-willed man should be automatically disqualified from church leadership.

---

[161] *The Message of 1 Timothy & Titus*, Stott, page 177.

Several years ago, I served as an overseer and mentor to some churches here in this area. One of the pastors that I worked with had a very difficult personality. I could never give him any advice or feedback. He was always right. He knew more and he knew better. Several other pastors talked to me and had the same nasty and sour experiences with him as well. Over the course of several years, many leaders left his church because they were beaten and wounded by this man's arrogance. Before we could intervene, he left our fellowship of churches and joined with another group. Recently, I heard from some leaders in his church that the church has gone through a dreadful church split

Never appoint self-willed elders!

People's views on money are important, especially when it comes to appointing them for leadership. Let's take a close look at that next.

16

The Church Leader Must Not Be Greedy for Money

"For a bishop must be blameless, as a steward of
God, not self-willed, not quick-tempered, not given to
*wine, not violent, **not greedy for money**."*
(Titus 1:7)

One of the main ministries an elderly widow can devote herself to is the ministry of prayer and intercession. Paul wrote in 1 Timothy 5:5, "Now she who is really a widow, and left alone, trusts in God and continues in supplications and prayers night and day." Recall that Anna was "a widow of about eighty-four years, who did not depart from the temple, but served God with fastings and prayers night and day."[162] Christians can "serve God" through prayer.

Over the years, I have recruited widows to be intercessors at our church. Elderly widows may not be able to do what they once did physically, but I found that all widows can pray.

That's why I put Helen in our group of intercessors. She was now in her early eighties. She was spiritually mature, well versed in the Scriptures, and a very reliable and faithful woman. She came to all the prayer meetings each week. On occasion, we did notice that she would forget some things and she also repeated the same stories regularly.

---

[162] See Luke 2:37.

Another important thing about Helen's life was that she also had a lot of money. She owned some properties and had a lot of cash in various banks.

For some unexplained reason, she started going to the bank every week and withdrawing $200. And she started giving me these $200 at the beginning of our prayer meetings.

She said, "This money is for you because I want to bless you as my pastor."

The first time she gave me the money, I was surprised, but I thanked her for her generosity.

However, she gave me $200 every week for a whole month. Now I started to get very uncomfortable. Finally, after the sixth week, I had $1,200 in cash in an envelope at my house. I decided to talk to the Lord about what was happening.

I'll never forget what He spoke to my heart.

"This was a test. I was testing you to see what you would do with her money. I wanted you to see just how much covetousness and love of money you had in your heart."

Wow! A fear of God came over me right at that moment. I was so glad I passed the test!

I immediately called Helen's daughter. I told her that I need to meet with her right away because I had something I wanted to give her.

She was not a member of our church, but she had visited on occasion, so she knew our location. I met her out in the parking lot.

"Hi Donna. Here is something I need to give back to you and your mom. Your mom has been giving me $200 every week for the last six weeks. The Lord told me to give it back to you."

Donna blushed and stared at the envelope with all the money. She told me later that she was shocked that a pastor would do that. She had a belief that many pastors were money-hungry and out to take advantage of people.

Donna then explained that her mom (Helen) had been recently diagnosed with dementia and the family may have to place her in a memory care facility soon. Within a week or two, Helen stopped attending our services. I did not see her again for the next ten years until she died at the age of ninety-two.

When Helen died, Donna called me. "I want you to officiate the funeral. I'll never forget what you did with my mom's money. Our family trusts you. Thank you for being her pastor for many years."

Without exaggeration, many millions of dollars have passed through my hands over the last nearly forty years – both personally and at church. Christians have handed me very large checks. I've received envelopes filled with hundreds and thousands of dollars in cash. One man handed me a check for $15,000 in our parking lot. Many temptations will come with money.

The church elder must not be greedy for money. This requirement is not only given for elders (Titus 1:7), but also for deacons (1 Timothy 3:8). Some translations have "not a lover of money," "free from the love of money," and the famous KJV, "not greedy of filthy lucre." The Amplified adds, "Insatiable for wealth and ready to obtain it by questionable means." He cannot be materialistic.

It is very interesting that just four verses later, Paul tells Titus about false teachers who "must be silenced, because they are turning whole families away from the truth by their false teaching. Such teachers are only after your money." One translation says, "They teach only to cheat people and make money." The Greek adjective used here at the end of Titus 1:11 is the same root word as used at the end of Titus 1:7. Both Greek words convey the idea of doing something "shameful" (aischros). It is a "gain" that is corrupt, "dirty," and venal. Barclay translates it, "he must not be a seeker of gain in disgraceful ways."[163] The church's elders cannot be greedy for money like the false teachers.

Peter told the elders to "serve as overseers – not because you must, but because you are willing, as God wants you to be; *not greedy for money*, but eager to serve" (1 Peter 5:2). Unfortunately, this is a great stumbling-block in many ministries today. It is terribly sad that many preachers tell their audiences that expensive cars, houses, and clothes are the model of true Christian success. *An elder who is greedy for money is not only*

---

[163] *The Letters to Timothy, Titus, and Philemon*, Barclay, page 265.

disqualified from ministry, he is also a cancer to the soul of his church. Paul would say in 1 Timothy 6:9-10, "But those who desire to be rich fall into temptation and a snare, and into many foolish and harmful lusts which drown men in destruction and perdition. For the love of money is a root of all kinds of evil, for which some have strayed from the faith in their greediness, and pierced themselves through with many sorrows." There are some awful words here – snare, foolish, lusts, drown, destruction, perdition, evil, strayed, greediness, pierced, and sorrows. All these words come with a love of money. There are many preachers in all parts of the globe who are "lovers of money." I guarantee that such a minister will use the church for his own means.

Peter also spoke of false ministers using these words: "Those false teachers only want your money, so they will use you by telling you lies" or "in their greed they will make up clever lies to get hold of your money." They are just like Balaam – "They have a heart trained in covetous practices." Balaam "fell in love with the money he could make by doing wrong."[164] Jude would say that "like Balaam, they deceive people for money" or "they will do anything for money."[165]

In Luke 16:13, Jesus said, "No servant can serve two masters; for either he will hate the one and love the other, or else he will be loyal to the one and despise the other. You cannot serve God and mammon." Knight is correct: "When a person serves money, he cannot serve God."[166] The very next verse reads, "Now the Pharisees, *who were lovers of money*, also heard all these things, and they derided Him." Do you become angry when someone talks to you about how you handle your money?

It is significant that the first mention of Christian elders in the book of Acts shows them receiving money for distribution among needy people (Acts 11:30). You need people of godly character to handle the Lord's money in a righteous manner.

Don't appoint elders in your church who are greedy for money. They will take advantage of God's people. So many

---

[164] See 2 Peter 2:3 and 2:14-15.
[165] See Jude 11.
[166] *The Pastoral Epistles*, Knight, page 292.

prosperity preachers have lined their pockets with money from Christian believers. A greedy elder will make money his priority.

Along these same lines, Paul teaches that an elder must not be covetous. These people have a strong desire to possess something that belongs to somebody else. Let's talk about that next.

17

The Church Leader Must Not Be Covetous

*"A bishop must not be given to wine, not violent, not greedy for money, but gentle, not quarrelsome, **not covetous.**"*
(1 Timothy 3:3)

According to Roman Catholic theology, the seven deadly sins are the seven behaviors that provoke further sin. They are pride, greed, lust, envy, gluttony, wrath, and sloth. This list was first proposed by Pope Gregory I in the 6th Century and later elaborated on by the Catholic theologian, Thomas Aquinas, in the 13th Century. Aquinas concluded that the two main sins were pride and greed. He called them "capital" sins after the Latin word, "caput," which means "head." They were later changed to "deadly" sins.

All dictionaries give "greed" and "covetous" the same definition. It is "an excessive desire, especially for wealth (money) or possessions." The Greek adjective that Paul uses for "not covetous" in 1 Timothy 3:3, "aphilarguron," means literally "a" (not) + "philarguros" (fond of silver). The NIV translates it as "not a lover of money" and most modern translations use "he must not love money." Paul wrote in 1 Timothy 6:10, "For the love of money (philarguria) is a root of all kinds of evil, for which some have strayed from the faith in their greediness, and pierced themselves through with many sorrows." The Pharisees "were lovers of money," and the last days will include many "men who will be lovers of themselves, lovers of money...lovers of pleasure rather than lovers of God."[167] They will love everything but God.

This requirement that an elder must not be covetous should be obvious. One of the Ten Commandments says, "You shall not covet." Jesus said that "covetousness" was "evil" and it "defiles a man." Paul wrote twice that "a covetous man" was "an idolater" and had "no inheritance in the kingdom of God and Christ." Several times, Paul listed "the covetous" along with other wicked people – "filled with all unrighteousness, sexual immorality, wickedness, covetousness, maliciousness; full of envy, murder, strife, deceit, evil-mindedness; they are whisperers, backbiters, haters of God, violent, proud, boasters, inventors of evil things, and disobedient to parents." We are commanded not to have any association with "covetous" people – not even to eat with them. Peter said that covetousness is the regular practice of false prophets and false teachers (like Balaam): "By covetousness they will exploit you with deceptive words" and "they have a heart trained in covetous practices, and are accursed children."[168]

Paul's personal testimony to a large group of elders included these words: "I have *coveted* no one's silver or gold or apparel." Jethro advised Moses to appoint leaders "such as fear God, men of truth, *hating covetousness*; place such over them." The wisdom of God teaches that "he who hates *covetousness* will prolong his days" or "will enjoy a long life." Jesus warned us to "take heed and beware of *covetousness*, for one's life does not consist in the abundance of the things he possesses."[169]

Finally, Achan and his whole family were stoned and burned with fire because of his covetousness; in his greed, Gehazi and all his future descendants were struck with leprosy; Balaam "ran greedily" after money and was killed by the sword; and the Lord was enraged with anyone who committed "the iniquity of covetousness."[170]

---

[167] See Luke 16:14 and 2 Timothy 3:2.

[168] See Mark 7:22-23; Ephesians 5:5; Colossians 3:5; Romans 1:29-30; 1 Corinthians 5:10-11; 2 Peter 2:3 and 2:14.

[169] See Acts 20:33; Exodus 18:21; Proverbs 28:16; Luke 12:15.

[170] See Joshua 7:21, 24; 2 Samuel 5:26-27; Jude 11; Numbers 31:8; and Isaiah 57:17.

"Throughout history, bad men have tried to make money out of the ministry."[171] All of us have seen the excesses and vices of televangelists (usually prosperity preachers) who milk people of their money and use it to buy expensive clothes, cars, houses, and even planes. Such false ministers offer people bottles of special anointing oil, books, or a reward from God for their "sowing." These people should be publicly rebuked and all true Christian believers should flee from these charlatans. One writer warns, "The man who desires to be rich wants to be rich quickly."[172]

But is this all Paul was addressing with this requirement of "not being covetous?"

No, there are some practical things that the church elder must be aware of that can subtly encroach upon his heart. Let me give three practical words of advice on covetousness based on three verses of Scripture that address the subject.

Hebrews 13:5 – *"Let your conduct be without covetousness; be content with such things as you have. For He Himself has said, 'I will never leave you nor forsake you.'"* Other translations begin with "keep your lives free from the love of money" or "don't fall in love with money."

One day I went to our local bank to talk to the General Manager. He is a Christian believer and I had worked with him for many years. Somehow, we got on the subject of loans.

"Did you know Pastor Charlie that banks charge churches some of the highest interest rates on loans?"

His question caught me off guard.

I asked, "Why is that?"

"Churches are notorious for defaulting on loans. They are very high risks for the banking industry, so we must loan them money at 8.9% interest, whereas other types of businesses are much, much lower."

He added, "And banks don't like to foreclose on churches because that makes the banks look bad. It appears that banks are

---

[171] *The Message of 1 Timothy & Titus*, Stott, page 97.
[172] From Juvenal, the Roman poet and satirist. Quoted by Calvin, page 56.

mean or even anti-Christian. Bank officers don't want that kind of reputation."

Over the years, I've met many church leaders and elders who are not content with what they have. They want "bigger and better" buildings and facilities. I'm convinced that in many cases, they didn't get their direction from the Lord but from their egos. In the Christian world of church growth and multiple campuses, elders are no different than the builders at Babel who simply "wanted to make a name for ourselves." Right after Jesus said, "Take heed and beware of covetousness, for one's life does not consist in the abundance of the things he possesses," He tells the parable of a "certain rich man" who tore down his smaller barns to build "bigger ones."

There are so many churches carrying hundreds of thousands or millions of dollars of loans borrowed from banks. Many of these churches are led by leaders who went to the banks and not the Lord. So many of these churches – often the larger ones – are living under tremendous burdens and pressures because of the heavy financial debts. Borrowers are slaves to lenders.[173] Truly, these churches are not free; they are bound.

The writer of Hebrews gives us a great word for today's elders – "be content with what you have." This is how to live "without covetousness." The same Greek adjective that Paul used in 1 Timothy 3:3 for elders is found here, and these are the only two places in the New Testament where the word is found. The reason we can live with contentment and without covetousness is because the Lord will never leave nor forsake us. "The Lord is my helper," so we don't "have to live in fear" (13:6).

Do we really need indoor basketball courts and five-million-dollar chapels for weddings and special events? I wonder how Paul and the other apostles made it without such elaborate facilities. Do you know how many native missionaries could be supported in the field with five million dollars?

Paul wrote, "I have learned to be content whatever the circumstances. I know what it is to be in need, and I know what it is to have plenty. I have learned the secret of being content in

---

[173] See Proverbs 22:7.

any and every situation, whether well fed or hungry, whether living in plenty or in want."[174]

Commenting on Hebrews 13:5, Knight says, "Contentment with God and His provision is commended as the antidote to love of money and the insatiable desire to get rich."[175]

The Lord told Jeremiah's scribe (Baruch), "Should you then seek great things for yourself? Seek them not." David said, "Lord, my heart is not haughty, nor my eyes lofty. Neither do I concern myself with great matters, nor with things too profound for me. Surely, I have calmed and quieted my soul, like a weaned child with his mother; like a weaned child is my soul within me."[176] Let us calm down and be content. Bigger is not always better if it means becoming slaves of others.

Proverbs 21:26 – *"The lazy man covets greedily all day long, but the righteous gives and does not spare."*

As an elder, you're going to be giving of your time, treasure, and talent all the time. The people at church will need and call on you at all hours of the day.

Jesus gave us such plain instruction: "Give to everyone who asks of you" and "if anyone wants to sue you and take away your tunic, let him have your cloak also. And whoever compels you to go one mile, go with him two. Give to him who asks you, and from him who wants to borrow from you do not turn away."[177]

Towner says that elders should be leaders who are "models of generosity and simplicity."[178]

I remember one time a lady in our church needed a vacuum cleaner. Her vacuum didn't work and was about thirty years old. A friend gave her an extra one that she had and it broke down right away. I saw one in the church closet that we were no longer using and gave it to her. She texted me the next day – "It's dead. It doesn't work." Finally, I just ordered one from Amazon and had it delivered directly to her house. My wife and I paid for

---

[174] See Philippians 4:11-12.
[175] *The Pastoral Epistles*, Knight, page 160.
[176] See Jeremiah 45:5; Psalm 131:1-2.
[177] See Luke 6:30; Matthew 5:40-42.
[178] *1-2 Timothy & Titus*, Towner, page 87.

it ourselves. It was a vacuum cleaner of good quality and it would last her for many years.

I didn't tell you that story to "do my alms before men." I tell you what did happen. Over the years, this lady had just about given up on all churches and pastors helping her. She concluded that most of them were hypocrites and unloving. That gift of a vacuum cleaner touched her heart so deeply, that she repented and started praising the Lord. Her attitude has never been the same.

In 1 Peter 5:2, the apostle addressed all elders: "Be shepherds of God's flock that is under your care, serving as overseers – not because you must, but because you are willing, as God wants you to be; *not greedy for money, but eager to serve.*"

Rather than take advantage of people financially, God's elders are always giving and not sparing as the proverb says. Like so many pastors and leaders, I have filled empty tanks with gas, bought groceries, paid for prescriptions, taken people food, shopped for clothes, paid utility bills, and given people rides to appointments and hospitals. Did I get taken advantage of on occasion? Yes. But I did it as unto the Lord. He knows my heart. I did it to bless, not curse. Many of these charitable actions were done in secret. Only the Lord knows, so only the Lord will reward. "You will be blessed, because they cannot repay you; for you shall be repaid at the resurrection of the just."[179]

Early on in my ministry, I determined that I wanted the same testimony as the prophet Samuel in 1 Samuel 12:3-4: "'Here I am. Witness against me before the Lord and before His anointed: Whose ox have I taken, or whose donkey have I taken, or whom have I cheated? Whom have I oppressed, or from whose hand have I received any bribe with which to blind my eyes? I will restore it to you.' And they said, 'You have not cheated us or oppressed us, nor have you taken anything from any man's hand.'" I love Paul's words – "Open your hearts to us. We have wronged no one, we have corrupted no one, we have cheated no one."[180] Let that be your testimony too.

When my life is over and I have finished my race, I don't want a single penny in my hand that I took from anyone by

---

[179] See Luke 14:14.
[180] See 2 Corinthians 7:2.

covetousness. Make up your mind right now that you will never take advantage of anyone financially – especially those under your spiritual care. You must stand before the Lord with clean hands.

1 Thessalonians 2:5 – *"Never once did we try to win you with flattery, as you well know. And God is our witness that we were not pretending to be your friends just to get your money!"* The NIV reads, "We never...put on a mask to cover up greed." This is "a cloak for covetousness" (NKJV).

The verses just before this verse say that Paul and his companions never used "any deceit or impure motives or trickery" (v3) in their preaching or appeals. Why? Because they were out "to please God and not men" (v4). They had been "entrusted with the glorious gospel," so all of their motives had to be pure. I love his words – "We NEVER put on a mask" just to get your money. God was witnessing everything so they could get away with nothing.

As elders, we will give an account to the Lord for how we handled His tithes, offerings, and other special gifts. His money must always be used for His glory and His purposes. The minute you start using it to enrich yourself and take advantage of others, you are living a lie.

Always be part of a church that has a responsible financial board or council that determines your salary and benefits (if you are paid as an elder). If you call all the shots and handle all the money yourself, you've opened the door to abuse. You are unaccountable, and covetousness will grip your heart.

The elder must not be covetous.

I would like to close this chapter with a beautiful line from the Psalms – "Incline my heart to Your testimonies, and not to covetousness," or as the NLT puts it, "Give me an eagerness for Your laws rather than a love for money!"[181] Amen.

---

[181] See Psalm 119:36.

18

The Church Leader Must Not Be Given to Wine

*"A bishop then must **not be given to wine**, not violent, not greedy for money, but gentle, not quarrelsome, not covetous."*
(1 Timothy 3:3)

*"For a bishop must be blameless, as a steward of God, not self-willed, not quick-tempered, **not given to wine**, not violent, not greedy for money."*
(Titus 1:7)

Before I received Christ into my life, I was a heavy drinker. I drank to get drunk. I lived in a fraternity in college where we had easy access to kegs of beer nearly every weekend. The living room of our fraternity house had a fully stocked bar of hard liquors. Also, my dad owned a bar and gambling joint while I was growing up.

Because of my past lifestyle of drinking and drunkenness, I made a decision before the Lord and in my heart that I would never drink again. I am free in Christ not to drink. Despite this choice I made privately with the Lord, I'm amazed at how many people have accused me of being legalistic and in bondage! What I praise the Lord for today is that His deliverance from beer, wine, and hard liquors was so complete, that since 1983, I have not even been tempted to drink again! It actually makes me nauseous when

I even smell any type of alcohol. What I used to love, I now hate. What a great victory for my life!

There are a lot of things the elder must NOT be – not a brawler, not soon angry, not violent, not greedy, not a novice, not self-willed, and not covetous. He must also not be given to wine.

The words, "given to wine," are one word in the original language. In the New Testament, it appears only in 1 Timothy 3:3 and Titus 1:7. It is the compound word, "paroinos," which is "para = near, besides," and "oinos = wine." It is someone who stays "near wine." Mounce defines it as "a person who spends too much time sitting with their wine."[182] It is variously translated as "not given to drunkenness," "not addicted to wine," or "not a heavy drinker."

Notice what Paul wrote to "deacons" and "older women" regarding drinking wine: "Likewise deacons must be reverent, not double-tongued, *not given to much wine*, not greedy for money" (1 Timothy 3:8) and "the older women likewise, that they be reverent in behavior, not slanderers, *not given to much wine*, teachers of good things" (Titus 2:3). These men and women are told not to drink "much wine."

I think Paul's words in Romans 14:21-22 are important: "It is better not to eat meat or *drink wine* or to do anything else that will cause your brother to fall (stumble). So whatever you believe about these things keep between yourself and God." A lot of opinionated people would benefit greatly by following the instruction in this last sentence. What I have observed over the years is that many Christians who don't drink usually condemn those who do, and Christians who do drink boast about their freedom in Christ to drink whatever they want. Paul wisely advised that whatever you believe about these things should be a private matter between you and the Lord. Paul knew it would be controversial.

So why would Paul bring up this qualification to both Timothy and Titus? Why should an elder not be "given to wine?"

Well, what would a young Christian be led to believe if he sees an elder (church leader) with a six-pack of beer in his refrigerator? What if a person who has been recently delivered

---

[182] See *Pastoral Epistles*, Mounce, page 175.

from drunkenness and received Christ comes to a pastor's house and sees a large collection of wines and liquors in his kitchen? Would this not be a stumbling block and open the way to trip up a young person or a former drunkard for whom Christ died? Beer and liquor have a *bad* association and the elder is called to a *good* work, who must have a *good* report with outsiders, be of *good* behavior, and be a lover of *good*. People are going to criticize you no matter where you stand on this issue, but I would rather be criticized for not drinking than for drinking. *No matter how free you are in Christ, it sets a bad example for the flock.*

Moses warned the priests in Leviticus 10:9, "Do not drink wine or intoxicating drink, you, nor your sons with you, when you go into the tabernacle of meeting, lest you die." It seems to me that it would be impossible to be a "drinking elder" and avoid criticism. The elder must be above reproach.

Stott makes this important point: "Alcohol is a depressant. It blunts and blurs our faculty of judgment. Those called to teach should take special warning. It is perhaps not an accident that 'not given to wine' should immediately follow 'an apt teacher.' Drinking and teaching do not go well together."[183] Towner adds, "The church cannot afford to be led by those who allow themselves...to inhibit decisive thinking."[184]

I remember asking a Christian these questions: At the next church fellowship or potluck on Sunday morning, would anyone be offended if you served coffee? The man answered, "No." What about if you offered punch or soft drinks like Coke, 7-Up, Dr. Pepper, and Pepsi? "Nope," he said. What if you made milk or hot chocolate available to the kids from Sunday School? "No problem," he responded. Well, what if you started pouring shot glasses of vodka, whiskey, cognac, and rum? What if you opened an ice chest full of Budweiser, Michelob, Coors, Corona, Heineken, and other popular beers? The brother got quiet. Finally, he said, "It would create a lot of problems and controversy." *If you can't bring it to church, it's probably not good for the church.*

---

[183] See *The Message of 1 Timothy & Titus*, Stott, page 98.
[184] *1-2 Timothy & Titus*, Towner, page 87.

Don't appoint church leaders who like to drink alcohol or speak favorably of those who do. You are going to open the door to lots of problems in your church. In many places, pastors and elders already have bad reputations. Let's not give our critics another reason to reject the gospel or the Lord because they see a beer bottle or a shot glass in our hand. Jerome, the Latin father, said, "Let your breath never smell of wine."[185] Remember, two of the requirements of elders are to be "temperate" and "sober-minded" (1 Timothy 3:2, Titus 1:8). "Let us watch and be sober. For those who sleep, sleep at night, and those who get drunk are drunk at night. But let us who are of the day be sober."[186]

The elder or "presbuteros" by definition is an older man. Let's see why he should not be a novice or inexperienced in the next chapter.

---

[185] See *Ancient Christian Commentary on Scripture*, Volume IX, page 171.
[186] See 1 Thessalonians 5:6-8.

19

The Church Leader Must Not Be a Novice

*"**Not a novice**, lest being puffed up with pride he fall into the same condemnation as the devil."*
(1 Timothy 3:6)

I think it is tremendously significant that 1 Timothy 3:6 and 3:7 each mention "the devil." *If you appoint unqualified men into your leadership, the devil will have easy access into your church.* Here in 1 Timothy, some people have "turned aside after Satan" (5:15), others have been "delivered over to Satan" (1:20), and here, Satan has been delivered over and turned over to us!

This is the only place in the New Testament where the word, "novice," appears. The Greek word is "neophutos," or "neophyte," which means "neo = new" + "phutos = planted." It is someone who is "newly planted." It simply means that an elder cannot be a new Christian, recent convert, or a beginner in the faith. No one should have problems understanding the reasons for this requirement. An elder needs to teach other people the Word of God and have a level of maturity that can bring balance, stability, and strength to the local body.

Promoting someone too soon is inappropriate and opens the door for a serious problem; namely, pride. If a novice gets into eldership, he will be conceited and his head will swell up.[187] Interestingly, the Greek word used here for pride (conceited) is used again a few chapters later in 1 Timothy 6:4 when Paul writes about false teachers who "are *proud*, knowing nothing, but are obsessed with disputes and arguments over words, from which come envy, strife, reviling, and evil suspicions." It is also found in 2 Timothy 3:4 when the apostle tells us of the defining sins of the "last days:" "Traitors, headstrong, *haughty*, lovers of pleasure rather than lovers of God." Other translations use "highminded," "puffed up," "conceited," or "inflated with self-conceit." Because of pride, the neophyte will come under the same condemnation as the devil.

Make no mistake about it – the proud devil will take advantage of a proud elder. You can never defeat the devil if you have the same nature as he does. And let us never forget the wisdom of Proverbs: "Pride goes before destruction, and a haughty spirit before a fall." Pride always causes people "to fall." Notice the wording again in 1 Timothy 3:6, "...with pride he will fall."

Many years ago, I had to wrestle with this qualification for church leadership. My pastor and our church appointed me as an elder in 1986. I was only twenty-six years old. I was single and had never married. Of course, I didn't have any children. I lived in an apartment and had never owned a house. I believe one of the reasons they appointed me as an associate pastor was because they saw I had a lot of zeal for the Lord and the work of ministry. I was eager to serve and, because I didn't have any family responsibilities, I made myself available at every opportunity. However, Proverbs says that "it is not good to have zeal without knowledge" and Paul wrote that unbelieving Jews "are zealous for God, but their zeal is not based on knowledge."[188]

---

[187] Kelly translates it, "swollen-headed." See *A Commentary on the Pastoral Epistles*, page 79. Barclay translates it, "...in case he becomes inflated with a sense of his own importance" (page 77). Yarbrough writes that "pride" or "conceit" "was used widely outside the New Testament to describe people who were overly impressed with their own knowledge" (page 201).

[188] See Proverbs 19:2 and Romans 10:2 in the NIV translation.

As a young elder, I found myself counseling troubled marriages even though I had never been married; giving advice on how to buy homes when I had never bought one; teaching concerned parents how to raise children when I never had any children. I always tried to counsel others with the Word of God, but I just didn't have the necessary experience to speak with much wisdom or authority.

However, Chrysostom gives some good advice so that not all young (in age) are disqualified: "The point is not that the bishop cannot be a young man but that he must not be a new convert, for if youth only was an objection, why did he himself appoint Timothy, a young man?"[189] This is a good point. Mounce agrees: "It cannot refer simply to a young person; otherwise, Timothy would be disqualified."[190] Joseph was only thirty years old when he began to rule all of Egypt. Jesus was thirty years old when He began His supernatural ministry. God used a young Joshua to help Moses and a young Elisha to help Elijah. I've seen many young men and young women do excellent work in ministry for the glory of God. As Paul will say in the next chapter of 1 Timothy, "Don't let anyone look down on you because you are young, but set an example for the believers in speech, in life, in love, in faith and in purity" (4:12). Young leaders can still set an example for all believers.

Let me give you three simple words of advice to encourage you to appoint elders who are older, more seasoned, and who have the necessary wisdom to impart to those in need.

First of all, Job said many important things about older people including this – "Wisdom belongs to the aged, and understanding to the old."[191] Our current associate pastor has been married for over fifty-five years. He's very disciplined and faithful. He and his wife have served the Lord for around forty years. He's a retired military officer. He has wisdom. He is very level-headed. His many life experiences help bring balance to my life. His steady presence in the church brings strength to everyone. Don't appoint novices.

---

[189] See *Ancient Christian Commentary on Scripture*, Volume IX, page 172.
[190] See *Pastoral Epistles*, Mounce, page 181.
[191] See Job 12:12, NLT translation.

Second, the law of God says, "You shall rise before the gray headed and honor the presence of an old man, and fear your God: I am the Lord."[192] Another translation reads, "Stand up in the presence of the elderly, and show respect for the aged." Proverbs 16:31 reads, "The silver-haired head is a crown of glory, if it is found in the way of righteousness." Recently, I saw a Bible teacher from Australia teaching a seminar in a local church. Most of the people in the audience were young people and young couples. The teacher had been serving the Lord faithfully for over seventy years. You could see how much this church respected this old man. It is vitally important that an elder be respectful. His wisdom, knowledge, and experience allow him to be admired and esteemed in a godly way. All churches need elders like this.

Finally, the Greek word for "elder" is "presbuteros." It means "an old man; elderly." In its various forms, presbuteros appears seventy-five times in the Greek New Testament. Zechariah told the angel, "I am an old man (presbutēs)." Paul said to "teach the older men (presbutēs) to be sober, reverent, temperate, sound in faith, in love, in patience." Paul himself told Philemon, "I then, as Paul – an old man (presbutēs) and now also a prisoner of Christ Jesus."[193] By definition, "elders" are "old men." Don't appoint novices. Don't appoint recent converts. Don't appoint those who are immature. Don't expose young men to the dangers of pride. Appoint older men who have been walking with the Lord for many years. Calvin's advice must be heeded: "Recent converts are not only bold and impetuous, they are full of self-confidence, and act as if they can fly beyond the clouds. It is a good idea not to make them bishops until later when their airy ideas have been subdued."[194]

It's now time to look at the church leader's family. This is of critical importance in the selection process for if a man cannot rule his own house, how will he rule the house of God? Let's study that next.

---

[192] See Leviticus 19:32.
[193] See Luke 1:18; Titus 2:2; Philemon 9.
[194] See *1&2 Timothy & Titus*, Calvin, page 57.

The Church Leader and His Family

- He must be the husband of one wife.

- He must rule his household well.

- He must have faithful (believing) children.

- He must have children who are obedient and respectful.

- He must not have children known to be wild and disobedient.

20

The Church Leader Must Be the Husband of One Wife

*"A bishop then must be blameless, **the husband of one wife.** "*
(1 Timothy 3:2)

*"If a man is blameless, **the husband of one wife.** "*
(Titus 1:6)

For various reasons, this is the most controversial qualification. Commentators will write one or two sentences on other requirements, but with this one, they can write four or five pages.

Literally in Greek, it reads that the elder must be a "one wife husband." One commentator uses, "a man of one woman."[195] It is variously translated as "he must have only one wife," "he must be faithful to his wife," or "he must be faithful in marriage." Barclay translates it, "he must have been married only once."[196] The apostle also gave this qualification for deacons: "Let deacons be the husbands of one wife" (1 Timothy 3:12).

I believe it is important to note that just after writing that the elder or bishop must be "blameless" or "above reproach," Paul gives this instruction – "the husband of one wife." He must be

---

[195] See *The Pastoral Epistles*, Knight, page 157.
[196] See *The Letters to Timothy, Titus, and Philemon*, Barclay, page 77.

blameless in his relationship to his one wife. He must be faithful to her and have a good reputation with his family, friends, and the church regarding his marriage. Any scandal associated with his relationship to his wife should disqualify him from church leadership. I like Strauch's words: "Marriage is the most probing test of man's character and beliefs. Therefore, a Christian marriage is one of the most powerful testimonies to the gospel's life-changing power. Conversely, ruined marriages among Christians have the greatest potential for bringing disgrace upon the Christian message and community."[197]

So, what's Paul really after with this requirement? I believe Towner moves us in the right direction: "So the point of the phrase is probably not how often one can be married, nor precisely what constitutes a legitimate marriage, but rather how one conducts oneself in one's marriage. The leader of the church must be a model of faithfulness in marriage."[198] Knight says that an elder must be "a man of unquestioned morality, one who is entirely true and faithful to his one and only wife."[199]

Any church leader – pastor, elder, bishop, evangelist, teacher, deacon, or prophet – must have a strong marriage. His marriage must be peaceful and united. He must be close to his one wife and be investing lots of quality time with her. He must be treating her with kindness, gentleness, and loving care. One international known pastor – after more than sixty years of ministry and marriage – once said, "You are going to treat the bride of Christ the way you treat your own bride." What you do at home will eventually show up at church. You'll begin to treat church members the way you treat your own wife. "The robust love for God and people that is the lifeblood of pastoral care should be fueled by the discipline and joy of married love in the pastor's personal life. If a candidate shows signs of loving his wife like Christ loved the church (Ephesians 5:25), this is probably what Paul wants Titus to look for."[200]

It is very interesting that Paul gave four qualifications for the elder's children, but only this one for his wife. It mentions

---

[197] See *Biblical Eldership*, Strauch, page 193.
[198] See *1-2 Timothy & Titus*, Towner, pages 85 and 225.
[199] Quoted by Stott in *The Message of 1 Timothy & Titus*, page 94.
[200] See *The Letters to Timothy and Titus*, Yarbrough, page 196.

nothing about how he treats her or about her spiritual life. It doesn't even say that she must be a "believing wife," although that is probably assumed.

Paul is not speaking here against polygamous marriages. It would be unthinkable to put someone in church leadership who had two or three wives. As Guthrie writes, "No Christian, whether an overseer or not, would have been allowed to practice polygamy."[201] He mentions nothing about being single, a widower, or divorced. Paul is completely silent on remarriage of any kind. The entire focus is on *"one wife."* Nothing more is emphasized. And Paul gives no qualifications for the elder's wife like the four qualifications he gave for the deacon's wife – "Their wives must be reverent, not slanderers, temperate, and faithful in all things" (3:11). Obviously, the elder's wife should practice all these things as well.

I maintain the firm belief that every church, ministry, fellowship, denomination, or ministerial association should have its own guidelines and policies for how to handle divorced or remarried believers who desire to be elders or bishops. We all have to work out our salvation with fear and trembling. We do need to show anyone aspiring to this high office a lot of grace and mercy regardless of their background, but we must also hold to the clear teaching of Paul that these believers must be blameless and above reproach. I do believe that mature singles and widowers who remarry believing wives can serve as elders as long as they meet all the other qualifications found in 1 Timothy 3 and Titus 1. Gordon Fee is surely right when he says, "A good look at the man's home life will tell much about his character and his ability to give leadership to the church."[202] May the Holy Spirit and the Word of God guide us as we qualify Christians for this "good work."

Obviously, the biggest area of concern of the "one wife" qualification is for those who have been divorced or remarried. There is no way around it – you will have to ask many questions and investigate carefully the circumstances of any divorce or remarriage.

---

[201] See *The Pastoral Epistles*, Guthrie, page 92.
[202] See *1 and 2 Timothy, Titus*, Fee, page 173.

For many years, I served as the licensing overseer for our area to interview and confirm new pastors and ministers. I appointed interviewing boards for these licensing candidates. We had separate interviews for those candidates who had been divorced or remarried.

Here is what you'll want to ask: What do you believe about the "one wife" requirement of elders? How do you interpret that verse considering your divorce? How and why did your first marriage end in divorce? Was your first wife a Christian? Were you a Christian believer during your first marriage? Can we interview (by phone) the pastor who married you? Can we interview your children that you had with your first wife? Can we interview any former in-law or neutral person who could give their honest opinion about your first marriage? How long have you been married to your second wife? Are there any unresolved issues from your first marriage? Is there any area of controversy that may disqualify you from serving as a blameless or above reproach elder?

While showing grace, we must never run from asking hard questions.

What practical things can an elder or bishop do to maintain strong ties of unity and oneness with his "one wife?"

Do things together every day. My wife and I walk together each morning. We need the exercise to maintain good health plus we interact and talk about many things while walking. Daily communication is so important to being like-minded.

Eat together at least once a day. Each pastor has a different schedule, but eating together with your wife is a key part of intimate conversation and interaction. Whatever you do, never eat alone with anyone who is not your wife. Only your *one* wife is your intimate companion. The word, "companion," means literally, "con" (with) + "pan" (bread). It is someone you eat bread (meals) with. Even our communion before the Lord involves the breaking of bread. My wife and I eat lunch together every day.

Pray together every day. My wife and I hold hands and pray together every night at 7:30pm. We also read from the Bible right after prayer. We usually read through the Bible using one-year reading plans or reading one chapter each night and discussing it. We're praying to the Lord together and we're talking about His Word together. This is a powerful spiritual binding that keeps you close to your "one wife."

In recent years, *I have found it exciting and joyful to take one week off each year to celebrate our anniversary.* Get away with the wife that you love. One of my favorite verses on marriage is Ecclesiastes 9:9 – "Enjoy life with your wife." Say that with me – "ENJOY LIFE WITH YOUR WIFE" (NIV). Go out of town. Get away from the daily grind of ministry life. Spend a week of quality time with her. My wife and I spend our "anniversary week" going to different parts of the United States and visiting new places. It's so much fun and it allows me to deliberately and purposely focus all my attention on my lovely bride. In the Song of Solomon, the woman's favorite words to hear from her man are "let's get away together."[203] Being alone for seven straight days does wonders for the closeness, intimacy, and love of your marriage relationship. Celebrate this special day when you made vows before God "until death do us part."

At the beginning of each new year, ask yourselves this question: What can we do together this year (daily, regularly) that will draw us closer together? Everything I've written in the last few paragraphs came into being when we asked ourselves this question during the first week of January each year. Pray, ask the Lord for direction and insight, then sit down and discuss what daily activity can be done to keep the fires of marital love burning brightly. This is very important.

Never forget – the most important instruction on marriage is Genesis 2:24. The two shall become one. Jesus quoted it in Matthew and Mark. Paul quoted it in Ephesians and 1 Corinthians. Stay close to your "one wife."

In the next four chapters, let's take a close look at the church leader's children and his household. The behavior, beliefs, and conduct of the elder's children reveal his ability to lead in the church. If he can't rule his own house, how will he rule God's house? "He who is faithful in what is least is faithful also in much; and he who is unjust in what is least is unjust also in much."

---

[203] See Song of Songs 1:4, 2:10, 2:13, 6:3, and 7:10-11.

121

21

The Church Leader Must Rule His Household Well

*"The bishop must be **one who rules his own house
well**, having his children in submission with all
reverence (for if a man does not know how to rule his
own house, how will he take care of the church of
God?)."*
(1 Timothy 3:4-5)

Jesus Christ teaches a very important principle in
Luke 16:10 that should be used to qualify Christians
for leadership positions in the church. It is a simple
truth, but one that holds great weight in the kingdom of God.

The Lord said, "He who is faithful in what is least is
faithful also in much." Another translation reads, "Whoever can
be trusted with very little can also be trusted with much." Both
the parables of the Talents and Minas also teach the same truth –
"Well done, good and faithful servant; you were faithful over a
few things, I will make you ruler over many things" and "well
done, good servant; because you were faithful in a very little, have
authority over ten cities."[204]

If you want to see how someone is going to handle matters
at the church, just look at how he is handling matters in his own
home. Paul tells us to really focus on the potential elder's

---

[204] See Matthew 25:21 and Luke 19:17.

children. Are they submissive? Are they God-fearing? Are they well-behaved? The conclusion is very logical – if he can't rule well over his small house, he will not be able to rule well over God's larger house. His management at home qualifies him for taking on greater responsibility. No one should question the wisdom of this requirement. As Paul told Timothy, "This is a faithful saying and worthy of all acceptance."

The key word found in both 1 Timothy 3:4 and 3:5 is the word "rule." Make no mistake about it – church elders and church leaders will rule. They will govern. They will be given authority and make decisions that will impact the life of the church and individuals. Paul will use the same Greek word in 1 Timothy 5:17, "Let the elders who *rule well* be counted worthy of double honor, especially those who labor in the word and doctrine," and as a requirement for deacons in 1 Timothy 3:12, "Let deacons be the husbands of one wife, *ruling* their children and their own houses *well*." The elders and deacons must "rule well" at home and "rule well" at church. Stott says, "The married pastor is called to leadership in two families, his and God's, the former is to be the training ground for the latter."[205]

Paul uses a compound Greek verb, "proistamenon," which is "pro" (before) + "histēmi" (to stand) or literally "to stand before." It is the leader who is out in front leading and guiding. In this context of 1 Timothy 3, it is the one who has been "set over" his own family and his church family. And this verb is a present tense, middle voice, participle; that is, the elder himself must continually be ruling his family well. He continues to be diligent and vigilant about the well-being of his family life.

Let's get right to the nitty-gritty. *If you want to see how an elder will rule in church, just look carefully at the behavior of his children.* Knight says that the children's subjection will "reflect the character of their father's leadership."[206] Titus 1:6 says that the elder's kids "must be believers who don't have a reputation for being wild or rebellious." Lenski writes, "Ill-trained, bad children reflect on any pastor, not merely because they are hurtful examples to the children of the members of the

---

[205] *The Message of 1 Timothy & Titus*, Stott, page 98.
[206] *The Pastoral Epistles*, Knight, page 161.

church, but still more because they show that the father is incompetent for his office."[207]

Do his children obey, respect, and submit to their dad? Are his children reverent and dignified? Are they rude, disrespectful, and talk back to people? Hebrews 13:17, speaking of elders, says, "Obey those who rule over you, and be submissive, for they watch out for your souls, as those who must give account." *Why should Christians be submissive to him at church when his own children are not submissive to him at home? He must be a good dad before he will ever be a good elder.* Guthrie makes the necessary point: "Any man unable to govern his children graciously and gravely by maintaining good discipline, is no man for government in the church. Lack of proper management of home-life disqualifies the person from leadership in the church."[208] Barclay's words are clear: "A man who had not succeeded in making a Christian home could hardly be expected to succeed in making a Christian congregation. A man who had not instructed his own family could hardly be the right man to instruct the family of the church."[209]

On a recent missions trip, I met a pastor who had been married for fifty-two years and had eight children. All of his children were involved with him in the work of the ministry or missions. He does not have to preach a sermon about good family life; his wife and children are the sermon! When this man speaks, people listen.

I cannot say this enough – all elders and church leaders must make their wives and children a priority over the ministry. If you take care of the one, the other will take care of itself. Never neglect your first ministry – the ministry to your wife and children.

I just talked to a young man who was bitter against the church. His dad spent nearly all of his spare time at the church doing church work and attending church events. This father spent almost no time with his own son. The son wanted nothing to do with church. He said he was an agnostic. This should never be.

---

[207] Quoted by Hiebert in *1 Timothy*, page 67.
[208] *The Pastoral Epistles*, Guthrie, page 93.
[209] *The Letters of Timothy, Titus, and Philemon*, Barclay, page 83.

Elders, the behavior of your children can make or break your ministry.

Paul gives all dads key insights on how to raise submissive children. We must not be hard with them. We must treat them with love, kindness, goodness, and gentleness. Colossians 3:21 reads, "Fathers, do not embitter your children, or they will become discouraged." The ERV says, "Fathers, don't upset your children. If you are too hard to please, they might want to stop trying." Ephesians 6:4, "Fathers, do not provoke your children to anger by the way you treat them. Rather, bring them up with the discipline (training) and instruction (admonition) that comes from the Lord."

Assuming a Christian is ruling well in his home, how can an elder "rule well" in "the church of God?" Let me give at least four things to consider.

Paul uses the same Greek word for "rule" (proistēmi) in 1 Thessalonians 5:12-13, "Now we ask you, brothers, to respect those who work hard among you, who *are over* you in the Lord and who admonish you. Hold them in the highest regard in love because of their work." Though it is not popular, one of the elder's most important tasks is to admonish or warn God's people. Paul warned the elders of Ephesus of wolves "night and day with tears." As Paul was preaching Jesus, he was "warning every man, and teaching every man in all wisdom; that we may present every man perfect in Christ Jesus." He said, "Warn those who are unruly." For the idle or lazy brother, he said, "Count him not as an enemy, but admonish him as a brother."[210]

Over the years, I've warned many Christians. They listened and received the blessings of God. I've also warned others who have not listened and they continued in their disobedience and suffered terrible consequences.

Many years ago, a single Christian man in our church showed up at one of the Sunday services with a woman I had never seen before. I found out after the service that she was married to a prominent psychologist in our city but had recently separated

---

[210] See Acts 20:31; Colossians 1:28, 1 Thessalonians 5:14; and 2 Thessalonians 3:15.

from him. When I met this lady at the service, I sensed a very strong spirit of lust on her.

That afternoon, I called the young man and asked if he could come to my house the next day, Monday.

When he came over, I told him what I was sensing and warned him to stay far away from her. I said to him bluntly, "If you don't stay away from her, you'll be in bed with her very soon." He swore that he would never do such a thing since she was still married to her husband.

Within one month, she was pregnant with this man's child. Some people listen but others don't. Regardless, elders must warn the people to live in obedience to God.

Secondly, when describing motivational gifts in the church, Paul again uses the same Greek word for "rule" (proistēmi) in Romans 12:8. In various translations, it reads, "he that ruleth, with diligence" (KJV), "if it is leadership, let him govern diligently," and "if God has given you leadership ability, take the responsibility seriously" (NLT). The key term is "diligence."

A dictionary defines "diligence" as "showing persistent and hard-working effort in doing something." The Greek word, "spoudē," includes the word, "haste" or "speed." Get on it right away. Don't wait around. Don't waste any time in getting to work. I find it interesting that spoudē is used a few verses later in Romans 12:11 where Paul writes, "Not lagging in *diligence*, fervent in spirit, serving the Lord." Don't be lazy. Be zealous. Be fervent. Don't hold anything back. Spoudē requires both zeal and seriousness.

For an elder, you must address problems right away. If a toilet is not working, get a plumber or a handyman on it right away. If the janitors are not doing their jobs cleaning the church, address it with them right away. Don't let rooms, trash cans, and restrooms be left dirty or overflowing with trash. If there are unresolved problems in the Sunday School or on the worship team, get on it now and talk to the necessary people. If a widow is being neglected, assign a responsible person to do follow up. Stay on top of things. Be alert. Be vigilant. Pay attention.

Some time ago, for several consecutive weeks, the church members who clean the church each week didn't even show up to clean the building. The restrooms needed toilet paper and paper towels. Old bulletins were in various parts of the sanctuary. The kitchen was overflowing with stuff. The classrooms for the children were disorganized. This was early Sunday morning!

I remembered what the Lord spoke to my heart years ago when I first started pastoring our church. *If you can't even make sure there's toilet paper in the bathroom, why should these people trust you to watch over their souls?* If you can't do what is least, you will not do what is much. Pay attention to details. Be diligent.

Needless to say, I cleaned some of the church myself and called one of the janitors who came over within one hour and he cleaned everything else before the service started. The physical condition of the church can often reflect the diligence of its leadership.

Third, the phrase, "those who have rule over you," is mentioned three times in Hebrews, Chapter 13 (verses 7, 17, and 24). He is speaking about pastors, elders, or overseers.

Hebrews 13:7 says, "Remember those who rule over you, who spoke the word of God to you. Consider the outcome of their way of life and imitate their faith." These last three words are rendered "follow the example of their faith" or "copy their faith" in other translations. People in your congregation are going to imitate what you do, especially in how you relate to the Lord. They are going to examine "the outcome of your way of life." The elder's lifestyle and faith will have tremendous influence in the church. It's like what Jesus said in John 5:19, "The Son can do nothing by Himself. He does only what He sees the Father doing. Whatever the Father does, the Son also does."

When our daughter started taking piano lessons as a young girl and then began to play the keyboard and guitar on the worship team, other mothers took their kids to get piano lessons. When we became foster parents and adopted a young boy, several other parents did the same thing. If you do things and they work well for you, your church members will copy you. People speak today of "social media influencers." Well, you're a spiritual influencer to those around you. Set a good example. Others are watching carefully "those who rule over them."

Finally, one of the most important responsibilities of those who rule in the church is found in Hebrews 13:17: "Obey those who rule over you, and be submissive, for they watch out for your souls, as those who must give account." Elders watch over souls. We are shepherds overseeing the flock. We are constantly looking out for wolves. We notice right away when someone is missing from the family/church gatherings. We are diligent to follow up.

Nearly always, I send a text message or call people who are missing from the Sunday services. "Hey, we missed you today. Hope you're doing okay. Let us know if you need anything." Sometimes people are sick, out of town, or have a prior commitment. This follow up lets the sheep know that you are keeping an eye on them. They are noticed.

We have a roster that includes the names, addresses, and phone numbers of all of our church members. Every week, I pray through this list, including all the teenagers and children. I'm amazed at how often the Lord leads me to call, text, or visit someone after praying for them. "Hi John, I was praying for you this morning and just want to see how you're doing. Let me know if you need anything or need prayer. God bless." I'm surprised how often these people are struggling with something when I contact them. Praying regularly for others is the best way to be a watchman on the watchtower overseeing people's souls. The Lord alerts elders to problems in prayer.

Let me close this important chapter with the words of Alexander Strauch in his excellent book, *Biblical Eldership*. This is a clear overview of what I wanted to communicate in this chapter.

"Caring for the local church is more like managing a family than managing a business or state. Therefore, a man's ability to manage God's church is directly related to his ability to manage his own household. A man may be a successful businessman, a capable public official, a brilliant office manager, or a top military leader, but a terrible church elder. In the family of God, a man's ability to lead his family is the test that qualifies or disqualifies a man to be an elder. An elder's relationship with his children will manifest itself in his relationship with the congregation. If he is too harsh with his children – rigid, impatient, insensitive, permissive, inconsistent, or passive – that is how he will respond to the congregation. If one wants to know what an elder will be like, observe how he manages his children."[211]

Let's look carefully in the next three chapters at the elder's children. They are such a critical part of the qualifications of a church leader. His children must be believers, submissive, respectful, and under control.

---

[211] *Biblical Eldership*, Strauch, page 202.

22

The Church Leader Must Have Faithful (Believing) Children

*"An elder must be blameless, the husband of but one wife, **a man whose children believe** and are not open to the charge of being wild and disobedient."*
(Titus 1:6)

One of my favorite verses for children is 3 John 4: "I have no greater joy than to hear that my children are walking in the truth." For the Christian parent, there is "no greater joy" than to see our children "continually walking in the truth."[212] The apostle John uses the emphatic Greek pronoun, "ema," which shouts out, "MY!" They don't belong to others; they are mine! *My* kids are living for God. This brings the greatest joy imaginable for the parent. Many verses in Proverbs attest to this truth: Proverbs 23:15-16 – "My son, if your heart is wise, my heart will rejoice – indeed, I myself; yes, my inmost being will rejoice when your lips speak right things." Proverbs 23:24-25 – "The father of the righteous will greatly rejoice, and he who begets a wise child will delight in him. Let your father and your mother be glad, and let her who bore you rejoice." Proverbs 29:3 – "Whoever loves wisdom makes his

---

[212] The Greek present tense participial verb (peripatounta) indicates that the children "keep on walking in the truth." It's a lifestyle, not a one-time occurrence.

father rejoice." One of the most joyful fathers in the New Testament was "Philip the evangelist" because "this man had four virgin daughters who prophesied."[213] His daughters were all full of the Holy Spirit. What parent wouldn't want that for his children?

Various translations of Titus 1:6 read: "His children must be believers," "his children must be faithful to God," "their children must be followers of the Lord," and "their children must love the Lord." Knight translates it, "a one-woman man, having believing children." He adds, "Paul now spells out what he means by being above reproach."[214] The Greek word for "faithful" (pistos) appears sixty-seven times in the New Testament and means either a born-again Christian believer or someone who is "faithful" to the Lord. Paul's use in many other letters clearly indicate someone who is saved and serving the Lord. For example, "What does a *believer* have in common with an unbeliever?" "For our hope is in the living God, who is the Savior of all people and particularly of all *believers*." "Let no one despise your youth, but be an example to the *believers*." "Those who have *believing* masters are not to show less respect for them because they are brothers."[215] Paul tells Titus "to appoint elders in every city as I commanded you...who have faithful (believing) children" (verses 5-6). The elder's children must be Christians. Hiebert asks, "If he is not able to win his own children to the faith, how will he lead others to the faith? The inability to train and govern a family creates a presumption of inability to train and govern the church."[216] Once again, "As in 1 Timothy, the home is regarded as the training ground for Christian leaders" or "their children provide a useful test of their suitability"[217] for church leadership.

Fee makes an insightful comment: "His children are themselves to be believers; that is, the potential elder is to be the kind of person whose children have followed him in adopting his

---

[213] See Acts 21:8-9.

[214] *The Pastoral Epistles*, Mounce, page 388.

[215] See 2 Corinthians 6:15; 1 Timothy 4:10, 4:12, and 6:2.

[216] *Titus and Philemon*, Hiebert, page 32. The second sentence is a quote from Harvey's commentary.

[217] *The Pastoral Epistles*, Guthrie, page 197; *A Commentary on the Pastoral Epistles*, Kelly, page 231.

faith."[218] Barclay adds, "He must be someone who has taught his own family in the faith. The Council of Carthage later laid it down: 'Bishops, elders, and deacons shall not be ordained to office before they have made all of their own households members of the Church.'"[219] Stott shows the evangelistic tone of this qualification: The elders "can hardly be expected to win strangers to Christ if they have failed to win those who are most exposed to their influences – their own children."[220]

Several commentators argue that "faithful children" means "loyal or trustworthy." One writes, "Paul does not set up a contrast between believing and unbelieving children. Even the best Christian fathers cannot guarantee that all their children will really believe. To say this passage means 'believing Christian children' places an impossible standard upon a father. Salvation is a supernatural act of God. God, not good parents (although they are used of God), ultimately brings salvation." This author then quotes John 1:12-13, "But as many as received Him, to them He gave the right to become children of God, to those who believe in His name: who were born, not of blood, nor of the will of the flesh, nor of the will of man, but of God."

It seems obvious to me that a Christian leader with children who are believers establishes a powerful example to the rest of the congregation. I really appreciate people who are loyal and trustworthy, but what does that matter in the end if they are not saved? John saw "unbelievers" (apistos) in the lake of fire. My hope is that my children and the children of all Christian leaders will have trustworthy kids who are also believers in Jesus.

I am well aware that this is the source of much anxiety and consternation among pastors and church leaders. Christian parents live in grief when their kids don't follow the Lord. Proverbs says, "A foolish son is the ruin of his father," "a foolish son is a grief to his father, and bitterness to her who bore him," "a foolish son is the grief of his mother," and "a foolish man despises his mother."[221] This is especially true for those who received Christ after their children become adults or those who have

---

[218] *1 and 2 Timothy*, Fee, page 173.

[219] *The Letters of Timothy, Titus and Philemon*, Barclay, page 263

[220] *The Message of 1 Timothy & Titus*, Stott, page 176.

[221] Proverbs 19:13, 17:25, 10:1, and 15:20.

adopted or become foster parents to troubled children.[222] Each case must be fully weighed with grace and truth. Even the great evangelist, Billy Graham, had adult children who divorced and used drugs. Should he be held responsible for their actions? This is always a tough question to answer as elders seek to live a blameless life. No doubt, the enemy wars against "PK's" (preacher's kids) to ruin the testimony of their parents. We must never fail to pray for the salvation of our children and that they will continue to walk in God's ways.

Let's share some practical thoughts on leading your children to faith in Christ and keeping them serving Him.

Tell your children about Jesus and His salvation. I raised my children with daily prayers and daily Bible readings at home. I led both of my children to the Lord in my house when they were young. I didn't wait until an evangelist came to town nor when he/she joined the youth ministry.

When my daughter was three years old, the Lord spoke to my heart about her "receiving Jesus in her heart." I brought her into my bedroom, talked to her about Jesus at a three-year-old level, and then asked her if she wanted to receive the Lord and serve Him. Of course, she immediately said "yes." I had her repeat a simple prayer and I laid hands on her. Within a few days, she began to have dreams about Jesus. I water baptized her at the age of six, and she has served the Lord all of her life.

The Bible teaches us, "Behold, the fear of the Lord, that is wisdom, and to depart from evil is understanding," "the fear of the Lord is the beginning of wisdom, and the knowledge of the Holy One is understanding," "the fear of the Lord is the beginning of wisdom," and "the fear of the Lord is the beginning of knowledge."[223] The foundation of all true education and learning is the fear of the Lord. To fear the Lord is to hate evil.

If you want your children to continue as Christian believers, you must put them in schools where they can be taught about God and His Word. Their education must be founded on the fear of the Lord. When we first got married, my wife and I

---

[222] I have written extensively elsewhere about the difficulties we endured while raising an adopted boy who was badly abused by biological family members.

[223] See Job 28:28; Psalm 111:10; Proverbs 9:10 and 1:7.

made the decision that we would put our children in Christian schools or homeschool them. We did both. Our daughter went to Christian schools from kindergarten to 10th Grade (until she ran out of classes). My son went to Christian schools for many years and I homeschooled him from 7th through 10th Grade. He completed 11th and 12th Grades at Fresno Christian High School and graduated from a Christian university. Today, both of our children are involved with local churches as musicians on worship teams. It was critical for their upbringing and development that they have Christian influences in their education. If you can do it (or afford it), put your children in schools or homeschool them in a Christian environment where the fear of the Lord is taught. So many of our young people get away from the Lord because they are constantly bombarded in schools with worldly beliefs that war against the truths of God.

1 Corinthians 15:33 reads, "Do not be deceived: 'Evil company corrupts good habits.'" The NIV says, "Do not be misled: 'Bad company corrupts good character.'" *If you want believing children, watch carefully who they have as friends.* Especially when they were young and as teenagers, we did not allow our children to have ungodly friends. We didn't see this as a matter of control, but as a matter of life or death. *Bad people ruin good character.* As a pastor, I have seen so many good Christian people court disaster because of the friends they associate with. The elder's children must be believing children. They must know the Lord and His Word.

Finally, *take your children on ministry assignments and outreaches.* Let them serve where you serve. I took my son regularly to homeless outreaches. He's helped me set up classes, sound systems, and video equipment at our church. I took my daughter with me so she could play the keyboard and lead worship before I taught. My daughter has gone on several missions trips with me. Both have helped me by leading worship with their instruments. Let your children serve alongside of you. Invest a lot of time into your children's ministry.

I close with Yarbrough's wise words: "Fit pastoral candidates, Paul is indicating to Titus, will reflect the grace of the gospel not only in love for their wives but in the kind of ties with their children that result in the latter's embrace of their parents' relationship with God, not their rejection of it. The children should 'believe.'"[224]

---

[224] *The Letters to Timothy and Titus*, Yarbrough, page 481.

23

The Church Leader Must Have Children Who are Obedient and Respectful

*"One who rules his own house well, **having children who are obedient and always respectful."***
(1 Timothy 3:4)

*"He must be a good leader of his own family. **This means that his children obey him with full respect."***
(1 Timothy 3:4, ERV)

The church leader must "rule" his family or house well. What does this mean? Paul says to take a good look at the behavior of his children. Various translations read, "…having his children in submission with all reverence," "…their children are obedient and always respectful," or "having children who respect and obey him." Barclay translates it, "…keeping his children under control with complete dignity."[225]

Paul uses two words to describe the conduct and manners of the elder's children. They must be "submissive" and "respectful."

---

[225] *The Letters of Timothy, Titus, and Philemon*, Barclay, page 77.

Paul had just used the Greek word for "submissive," "hupotagē," in 1 Timothy 2:11 when he wrote, "Let a woman learn in silence with all *submission*." It was a military term used for soldiers who were given orders from commanding officers. They were expected "to submit" to these orders and be obedient. One translation of this word is "being completely willing to obey." The elder's children must be obedient children. "Hupotagē" is a word focused on *authority*. Are his children submissive to his authority and others in authority? Stott writes, "Although pastoral ministry is a servant ministry characterized by gentleness, a certain authority also attaches to it. One cannot expect discipline in the local church if pastors have not learned it in their home."[226]

Guthrie comments: "Any man unable to govern his children graciously and gravely by maintaining good discipline, is no man for government in the church. Lack of proper management of home-life disqualifies the person from leadership in the church. It is important for a leader to command the respect of his children as well as commanding the respect of others."[227]

I spent five years of my life as an officer in the United States Air Force. As a captain, I had to report to my superiors both civilian and military. I often gave briefings to generals and senior executives in our chain of command. I also presented technical briefings at the Pentagon to senior officers. I once gave a briefing to a former boss, now a four-star general, concerning problems we were having with equipment used on F-15 and F-16 aircraft. There was a lot of pressure! Whenever they gave an order, I had to say, "Yes, sir!" It got done right away. Those who have been in the military understand authority. Like the centurion military officer told Jesus: "For I also am a man under authority, having soldiers under me. And I say to this one, 'Go,' and he goes; and to another, 'Come,' and he comes; and to my servant, 'Do this,' and he does it."[228] This is exactly the sense of the word, "submissive," here in 1 Timothy 3:4. *We obey right away!*

The second word, "semnotētos," means "reverent," "respectful," "dignified," or "serious(ness)." Knight highlights

---

[226] *The Message of 1 Timothy & Titus*, Stott, page 98.
[227] *The Pastoral Epistles*, Guthrie, page 93.
[228] See Matthew 8:9 or Luke 7:8.

this important point: "And note that this needs to be not just an appearance of 'semnotetos,' but 'pases semnotetos,' a full demonstration of it" (pases means "all"). The NKJV translates it, "...*all* reverence."

Paul will use it again in a few verses to describe deacons, "Likewise deacons must be *reverent*..." (3:8); deacon's wives, "likewise, their wives must be *reverent*..." (3:11); and in Titus 2:2 for the older men, "the older men must be sober, *reverent*..." Some translations render it, "worthy of respect," "respected by others," "serious," or "grave." It carries the idea of someone who is well respected because he is serious, level-headed, and has a dignified bearing. They speak with wisdom. They command the respect of others. "The subjection shown by the children must reflect the character of their father's leadership."[229]

Using the same Greek word, Paul told Titus that our "doctrine" or "teaching" should "show integrity, *reverence (seriousness, NIV)*, incorruptibility, sound speech that cannot be condemned, that one who is an opponent may be ashamed, having nothing evil to say of you."[230] Our doctrine must be presented in such a way that it garners respectability. Truth must be obeyed.

The truth is, the Lord commands all children, especially those in Christian households, to be obedient to their parents. Paul wrote, "Children, obey your parents in everything, for this is well pleasing to the Lord" and "children, obey your parents in the Lord, for this is right." The wisdom of God says, "My son, keep your father's command, and do not forsake the law of your mother." The prophet of God said, "A son honors his father." The law of God reads, "Every one of you shall revere his mother and his father." The Ten Commandments included, "Honor your father and your mother, that your days may be long upon the land which the Lord your God is giving you."[231]

What was expected of the elder's children is expected of *all* children. This requirement is not something unusual.

In the *Book of Common Prayer*, candidates for church leadership (the Anglican priesthood) are asked: "Will you be

---

[229] *The Pastoral Epistles*, Knight, page 161.
[230] See Titus 2:7-8.
[231] See Colossians 3:20; Ephesians 6:1; Proverbs 6:20; Malachi 1:6; Leviticus 19:3; Exodus 20:12.

diligent to frame and fashion your own selves, and your families, according to the doctrine of Christ, and to make both yourselves and them, as much as in you lieth, wholesome examples and patterns to the flock of Christ?"[232]

How can the truth of 1 Timothy 3:4 be lived out on a practical level?

First of all, I've learned that obedience and submission only works well if it comes from the bottom up, not the top down. If you must beat or force people into submission, it nearly always turns into disobedience and rebellion.

Did you notice that all the commands within families to submit and obey in the New Testament were from the bottom up? Never does Paul say, "Husbands, demand that your wife submit to you." Nor does he write, "Fathers, force your children to obey you." No, the instruction is always given to the one who needs to submit. Masters are never told to beat servants into submission. The command is always given to the servants – "Bondservants, be obedient to those who are your masters…with fear and trembling, in sincerity of heart, as to Christ" and "bondservants, obey in all things your masters, not with eyeservice, as men-pleasers, but in sincerity of heart, fearing God."[233]

I suppose all fathers have used anger or control to get our children to obey. It never works well. The command to "honor your father and mother" was given to children.

So, husbands never have to tell wives to submit; fathers never have to demand children to obey; masters never have to beat servants into submission. Why? *Because God has already told them to do it.* Obedience and submission only work from the bottom up. You do not need to command obedience from those under you because God has already done so.

And, by the way, you will take this same attitude and belief into the local church. No elder or pastor has to force church members to obey or submit to his authority. It is already written in God's Word. "Obey your leaders and submit to their authority. They keep watch over you as men who must give an account. Obey them so that their work will be a joy, not a burden, for that

---

[232] Quoted by Kelly, page 78.
[233] See Ephesians 6:5 and Colossians 3:22.

would be of no advantage to you." "Respect those who work hard among you, who are over you in the Lord and who admonish you. Hold them in the highest regard in love because of their work."[234]

Second, I believe the truth of "whatever a man sows that will he also reap" applies everywhere including here. If you sow obedience and submission into your marriage and your family, you will reap obedience and submission. What do I mean?

Before I leave the house, I always tell my wife and children where I am going and how long I will be gone. "I'm going to the hospital to see one of our church members. I'll be back in about two hours. I'll call if I'm delayed." This accountability and submission are communicated to the whole family. I noticed that as I started doing this many years ago, everyone in the family started doing it, even as my kids grew older and became adults. If I can use this metaphor – submission by the head of the house got into the rest of the body. Fathers should set the example that children can follow.

I hear so many troubles in marriages and families because husbands and wives, parents and children, are unaccountable. Where are they? They are not submissive. This secrecy opens the door to evil suspicions and negative thoughts.

Fathers, show your children how to submit by being submissive yourself. Set the example that they can follow. As Calvin said, "Children are likely to reflect their father's disposition."[235]

Finally, I wish I had learned this lesson when I first got married: Our children are in desperate need of encouragement and strength. I was too rigid and strict. I made many things too hard for my children. I wish I would have shown a lot more grace and mercy. Why was I putting them down when I should have been building them up? "Fathers, do not provoke your children, lest they become discouraged."[236]

Today, I receive the correction of 1 Thessalonians 2:11-12 – "For you know that we dealt with each of you as a father deals with his own children, encouraging, comforting and urging

---

[234] See Hebrews 13:17 and 1 Thessalonians 5:12-13.
[235] *1 & 2 Timothy & Titus*, Calvin, page 57.
[236] See Colossians 3:21.

you to live lives worthy of God, who calls you into His kingdom and glory." I believe this is one of the main ways that your children will respect and submit to you – always seek to encourage them in the ways of the Lord. They are already dealing with so many negative things in this world.

Recently, I counseled a young person who was being beat down by his Christian parents. He was looking for support, but all he was receiving was condemnation. I was amazed at how he came to life when I gave him words of encouragement. It's one of the reasons why I'm writing these words to you now. Paul wrote, "I may seem to be boasting too much about the authority given to us by the Lord. But our authority builds you up; it doesn't tear you down. So I will not be ashamed of using my authority" and "for I want to use the authority the Lord has given me to strengthen you, not to tear you down."[237]

Children respond much better to encouragement than criticism. Speak words of life, not death.

---

[237] See 2 Corinthians 10:8 and 13:10.

24

The Church Leader Must Not Have Children Known to Be Wild and Disobedient

*"An elder must be blameless, the husband of but one wife, **a man whose children** believe and **are not open to the charge of being wild and disobedient.**"*
(Titus 1:6)

I will never forget this pastor. He was young, handsome, and had a powerful and outgoing personality. He had a beautiful wife, several nice children, and a growing church. Every time we were around him, he told us of all the people who were receiving Christ. Everything about his personality exuded life and vitality. Whenever I drove by his church, the parking lot was full. The revival at his church was the talk of the town.

Suddenly, everything changed. Suddenly, there was silence. We no longer saw the pastor anywhere. He no longer came to the monthly gathering of pastors. The parking lot at his church was now half empty. Something was wrong. What happened?

Word leaked out that his fourteen-year-old daughter was pregnant. This was devastating news! We all knew how much he loved his family. His young daughter was the apple of his eye.

Not him! This was totally unexpected. All of us could feel the pain. What would happen next?

"This is the most devastating and overwhelming situation I have ever endured," he told us later. "The pain is unbearable. My wife and I have died a thousand deaths!"

We also learned that the hardest thing for him to handle was the public humiliation and shame. The cause and the witness of Christ were now tainted in that family and in that church. Everything that he preached and stood for all seemed very empty now. The pastor was big on family values. He taught much on purity and holiness in the lives of Christians. That verse in Ecclesiastes was so real: "One sinner can destroy much that is good."[238]

There was nowhere to run and hide. It was all very visible and out in the open. You cannot hide a pregnancy. It will eventually become known.

After the dust cleared, his biggest tormentor became a question. *Should he resign as pastor of the church?* Everything that he had worked for; everything that he had gone to school for; everything that he had known in life and ministry was on the brink. What was this pastor to do?

Other troubling questions waited for difficult answers. Who was the father? How did it happen? Would she come to church services with a baby bump while her dad preaches? What will the pastor-father tell the school where she was a student? How do you deal with all the raw emotions of condemnation, disgrace, and shame? What did the Lord think about all this?

This true story happened in a Midwest city back in the 1980s. I lived in that city for seven years. It was before gay marriage, transgenders, and the LGBTQI movement. The people were conservative. They honored family values. This truly was a scandal. Some Christians called it "an outrage."

The talk of the town was no longer the revival at the church but the pregnant fourteen-year-old daughter at the house! What a difficult trial!

Paul wrote in Titus 1:6, "An elder must be blameless, the husband of but one wife, a man whose children believe and are

---

[238] See Ecclesiastes 9:18, NLT.

not open to the charge of being wild and disobedient." Calvin says, "The person who cannot gain any respect from his own children will hardly be able to curb his people with the bridle of his discipline."[239]

Recall that earlier in this book, starting at chapter 12, we stated eight qualifications that must not be in an elder's life – NOT quarrelsome, NOT violent, NOT soon angry, NOT self-willed, NOT greedy for money, NOT covetous, NOT given to wine, and NOT a novice. He must also NOT have children who are accused of being wild and disobedient.

The church leader's children cannot have an accusation, charge, or reputation of being wild and rebellious. The Greek word here for "accused" or "charged" is a word we all know in English. It is a "category." The "katēgoria" was derived from the "agora" (the marketplace) where someone made a statement against another. It was a public condemnation. It was a criminal charge. In other words, it was known by many. One translation of Titus 1:6 reads, "They must not be *known* as children who are wild and don't obey."

Interestingly, Paul also used "katēgoria" in 1 Timothy 5:19: "Do not entertain an *accusation* against an elder unless it is brought by two or three witnesses." The bad behavior of an elder's children can bring "an accusation" against him. The only other place this Greek noun is used is in John 18:29, "Pilate then went out to them and said, 'What *accusation* do you bring against this Man (Jesus)?'"

The elder's kids cannot be "wild" or given to "riot" (KJV) or "dissipation" (NKJV). English dictionaries define the word, "dissipation," as "overindulgence in pursuit of physical pleasures; wasteful use or squandering of resources such as money." As I reflect on this definition, I think of the prodigal son in Luke 15. The connection can be made because the Greek noun here for "wild" (asōtia, literally, "inability to save"), appears in Luke 15:13 as an adverb, "asōtōs" – "A few days later this younger son packed all his belongings and moved to a distant land, and there he wasted all his money in *wild living*." One commentator defines "asōtia" as "the person who is wasteful,

---

[239] *1 & 2 Timothy & Titus*, Calvin, page 182.

extravagant and incapable of saving, and spends everything on personal pleasure. Such a person loses it all and, in the end, suffers personal ruin."[240]

"Asōtia" appears also in Ephesians 5:18, "And do not be drunk with wine, in which is *dissipation*; but be filled with the Spirit" or "do not get drunk on wine, which leads to *debauchery*. Instead, be filled with the Spirit" (NIV). Here, the word is associated with drunkenness.

The church leader's children must also not be "anupotakta." This is translated as "rebellious," "disobedient," "unruly," or "insubordination." It is a Greek word that means someone "who will not submit." This is the exact opposite of what we just saw in the last chapter from 1 Timothy 3:4 that the elder's children must be "obedient." Here in Titus 1:6, Paul uses the same Greek word for "obedient" but adds the negative Greek particle (a) or "disobedient." Amazingly, he uses the same Greek adjective four verses later to describe the false teachers: "For there are many *rebellious* people, mere talkers and deceivers, especially those of the circumcision group" (1:10). How can the elder's children behave just like false teachers? Paul uses the word again in 1 Timothy 1:9 to identify those who were not righteous: "We also know that law is made not for the righteous but for lawbreakers and *rebels*, the ungodly and sinful, the unholy and irreligious; for those who kill their fathers or mothers, for murderers."

I want to stop right here and look at the overall picture of an elder's home. Paul said in Titus 1:6 to "appoint" them only "if a man is blameless," and again in Titus 1:7, "for a bishop must be blameless." If his children are "wild and disobedient" it will be impossible to be blameless in the eyes of others. Stott says, "It is a solemn thought that parents are held responsible for the belief and behavior of their children."[241]

I would like to close this chapter with a brief look at some people in the Bible who were leaders but had children that were "wild and disobedient." Perhaps we can learn some important lessons for church leaders as we consider some biblical examples.

---

[240] *The Letters to Timothy, Titus, and Philemon*, Barclay, page 264.
[241] *The Message of 1 Timothy & Titus*, Stott, page 176.

The prophet Samuel and his sons.

Anyone reading the Bible's account of Samuel the prophet would conclude that he was a powerful man of God. He had a supernatural birth through his mother, Hannah (1 Samuel 1), and even as "a child" and as "a boy," "he ministered to the Lord," "Samuel grew before the Lord," and "Samuel grew in stature and in favor both with the Lord and man." He heard the Lord's voice. God's word came to him many times. 1 Samuel 3:19-21 gives a good summary of his call and ministry: "So Samuel grew, and the Lord was with him and let none of his words fall to the ground. And all Israel from Dan to Beersheba knew that Samuel had been established as a prophet of the Lord. Then the Lord appeared again in Shiloh. For the Lord revealed Himself to Samuel in Shiloh by the word of the Lord." Everyone – "all Israel" – knew he was a prophet of God.

He prayed and "the Lord thundered with a loud thunder." He judged Israel with wisdom and justice. He operated in supernatural gifts of prophecy and words of knowledge (revealing where Saul's donkeys were). Powerful outpourings of the Holy Spirit happened around him. He rebuked King Saul and anointed King David. He had such an impeccable testimony before the Israelites that no one could bring any charge of cheating or oppression against him.

And yet, his two sons, Joel and Abijah, "did not walk in his ways; they turned aside after dishonest gain, took bribes, and perverted justice." Even "all the elders of Israel gathered together and came to Samuel at Ramah, and said to him, 'Look, you are old, and your sons do not walk in your ways.'"[242] Interestingly, at no point did the Lord disqualify Samuel as a prophet because of the wild behavior of his sons. Israel, however, rejected his sons from becoming judges or kings over them.

We may never fully understand why Samuel's children turned out the way that they did. The Bible never explains why. However, we do know that from the time he was very young, Samuel was left at the tabernacle with Eli the priest. And Eli was a disastrous father as we will see next. Perhaps Samuel raised his kids just like Eli did. Maybe Samuel was so busy judging Israel

---

[242] See 1 Samuel 8:3-5.

and prophesying to many that he never took time for his children. Whatever the reason, I do believe we can say that Samuel learned parenting skills from Eli. This was not good.

I was not raised in a Christian home. I became a Christian believer five years after I left home and went to college. My father was married four times and fathered nine children from these women. He was a very hard worker and a strict disciplinarian. He showed very little love and emotion. Because he did not know Christ, I was never taught how "to train children in the nurture and admonition of the Lord."

As a young man of about twenty-four years old, I did find a Christian man who took me under his wing and trained me on how to raise children for the Lord. He brought me into his house and showed me all the practical ways of how he disciplined and taught his four children. He didn't use the pulpit or sermons; he taught me right in his own kitchen, living room, and bedrooms. I saw what he did, and that was all the example I needed.

Perhaps you have a similar story. Maybe you were raised by unsaved parents and were never taught the Word of the Lord or the fear of God as a kid. *If you are an aspiring elder, let me strongly encourage you to find an older couple in your church that has been walking with the Lord for many years and who have good, respectable children who are serving Jesus.* Meet with them. Learn what they did. Don't live in the dark. Get the necessary practical training that is so important today.

Eli the priest and his sons.

Eli was a priest who ministered before the ark of the covenant at the tabernacle of the Lord in Shiloh. He had two sons, "Hophni and Phinehas," who were also priests.

Over and over again, we are told about the wickedness of these two sons. "Now the sons of Eli were corrupt; they did not know the Lord," "the sin of the young men was very great before the Lord, for men abhorred the offering of the Lord," "he heard everything his sons did to all Israel, and how they slept (had sex) with the women who assembled at the door of the tabernacle of meeting. So he said to them, 'Why do you do such things? For I hear of your evil dealings from all the people.'" Because of how they treated God's offerings and God's people, "it was the Lord's will to put them to death" and God cursed Eli's family line so that "there would not be an old man in your house forever."[243]

I believe the key to Eli's failure as a parent can be found in 1 Samuel 2:29-30. "A man of God" approached Eli and asked the convicting question: "Why do you honor your sons more than Me?" He added, "Those who honor Me I will honor." Rather than obey God, Eli pleased his sons. He didn't want to hurt their feelings. Rather than listen to God, he listened to his sons. It was like what Paul said, "Am I now trying to win the approval of men, or of God? Or am I trying to please men? If I were still trying to please men, I would not be a servant of Christ." John also wrote, "They loved the praise of men more than the praise of God." Jesus said, "No wonder you can't believe! For you gladly honor each other, but you don't care about the honor that comes from the One who alone is God."[244]

We've all made mistakes raising our children. We've all had to be corrected and rebuked for our sin and anger. We've all done things that we regret. However, you must never compromise the glory, honor, and righteousness of the Lord. Speak the truth in love. Jesus is the "Rock of Offense," and He offended people many times with the truth. Paul asks, "Have I therefore become your enemy because I tell you the truth?"[245] Hopefully, our children won't turn against us. We must always seek to honor God before all others, even our children. You don't have to be mean and nasty; it just means that you won't compromise God's Word. "If you honor Him, He will honor you." And if God is for you, who can be against you?

David the king and his son, Adonijah.

David's fourth son was a man named "Adonijah." His mother's name was "Haggith." He was next in birth order after Absalom. He was "very handsome" or "very good-looking." He was the playboy in David's house. He probably spent hours working on his hair, ironing his clothes, and perfuming his body. David's grave error with Adonijah was that he never corrected him. He let him do whatever he wanted. He never "interfered" in

---

[243] The references in this paragraph include 1 Samuel 2:12, 2:17, 2:22-23, 2:25 and 2:31-32.
[244] See Galatians 1:10; John 12:43 and 5:44.
[245] See Galatians 4:16.

his life. The fruit of this type of upbringing was that he rebelled against David and Solomon by wanting to take the throne. He also lusted after "Abishag the Shunammite."

1 Kings 1:6 reads, "Now his father, King David, had never disciplined him at any time, even by asking, 'Why are you doing that?'" Some translations say that David "never corrected," "never interfered," "did not rebuke," or "did not displease" his son. The CEV ends with this pathetic observation: "David did not want to hurt his feelings, so he never asked Adonijah why he was doing these things." Proverbs 29:15 says, "The rod and rebuke give wisdom, but a child left to himself brings shame to his mother." Adonijah was "left to himself."

The tragic end of Adonijah's life happened when "King Solomon sent Benaiah son of Jehoiada to strike him down."[246]

In reading through the book of Proverbs, this instruction seems so obvious. *We must discipline our children. We must discipline them with the rod.* "He who spares his rod hates his son, but he who loves him disciplines him promptly." "Discipline your children while there is hope. Otherwise you will ruin their lives." "Foolishness is bound up in the heart of a child; the rod of correction will drive it far from him." "Do not withhold correction from a child, for if you beat him with a rod, he will not die. You shall beat him with a rod, and deliver his soul from hell." "The rod and rebuke give wisdom, but a child left to himself brings shame to his mother." "Correct your son, and he will give you rest; yes, he will give delight to your soul."[247]

I hate child abuse. I hate abortion. I hate the sexual abuse and exploitation of children.[248] My adopted son was abused by many different people, including his biological mother.

Godly child discipline with a rod (paddle) is not child abuse![249] It is wisdom directly from God. The verses above teach that if you don't discipline your son, you hate him. If you really

---

[246] See 1 Kings 2:25.

[247] See Proverbs 13:24, 19:18, 22:15, 23:13-14, 29:15 and 29:17.

[248] Some may be surprised by my use of the word, "hate." The Bible says "to hate what is evil." See Psalm 97:10; Proverbs 8:13; Amos 5:15; and Romans 12:9.

[249] When I was in elementary school in the 1960's, the principal used to discipline kids with a wooden paddle in his office.

love him, you'll discipline him promptly. The only way to drive out foolishness from the heart of your child is through the rod of correction. If you paddle him, he's not going to die! To the contrary, you're going to deliver his soul from hell! Strong words. When you correct your son, it gives him wisdom and it gives you rest.

David did not discipline his son, Adonijah. Eli refused to discipline his children, Hophni and Phinehas. All these children grew up to be rebellious, sexually immoral, and they led others astray. Eli honored his kids more than he honored his Lord.

Let us learn these valuable lessons from three fathers who did it wrong. Let us raise our children in the instruction and admonition of the Lord. They should not be wild and disobedient.

Let us now go to the final section of this book. Let's look at the church leader's main ministry. He must be able to teach God's Word. He will use the Scriptures to encourage people and refute those who are in error.

25

The Church Leader Must Be Able to Teach

*"A bishop then must be blameless, the husband of one wife, temperate, sober-minded, of good behavior, hospitable, **able to teach.**"*
(1 Timothy 3:2)

Notice carefully what we have covered so far: Nineteen qualifications for eldership involve his CHARACTER; five deal with his FAMILY (his wife and children); and the last three concern his MINISTRY. When qualifying leaders, many churches and pastors put nearly all the emphasis on a person's ministry (ability, giftedness, anointing). However, according to God's Word here in 1 Timothy and Titus, your main priorities should be to examine carefully his character and his family. If he is disqualified in these two critical areas, it doesn't really matter how well he can speak or teach. "No intellectual power or pulpit brilliancy can atone for the lack of solid Christian virtues and a blameless life."[250]

The last two chapters of this book center around the ability to teach others the Word of God (sound doctrine) and refute those who are in error. Let's start with the basic qualification – the ability to teach Scripture.

---

[250] *Titus and Philemon*, Hiebert quoting Harvey, page 37.

The Greek adjective Paul used in 1 Timothy 3:2 for "able to teach" is "didaktikon." It is where we get our English word, "didactic," which means "fond of instructing or advising others." One translation renders it, "He must be a good teacher." The only other place in the New Testament where this word appears is 2 Timothy 2:24, "A servant of the Lord must not quarrel but be gentle to all, *able to teach*, patient." The church leader must possess an aptitude for teaching. Kelly uses "a skilled teacher,"[251] the BAGD lexicon, "skillful in teaching," and the NRSV translation uses "an apt teacher." Hiebert defines "didaktikon" as "the willingness and the skill or ability to teach. The ability to teach implies the qualification of having himself been taught."[252] He also quotes Lenski: "The more a faithful teacher teaches, the more will he feel the need of acquiring more and more knowledge of the blessed truth he is to teach."[253]

Paul was not only an apostle; he was also a teacher. A few verses before 1 Timothy 3:2, he wrote, "For which I was appointed a preacher and an apostle – I am speaking the truth in Christ and not lying – *a teacher* of the Gentiles in faith and truth" (2:7). He will say it again in 2 Timothy 1:11, "...to which I was appointed a preacher, an apostle, and *a teacher* of the Gentiles."

Sixty-three times – more than any other ministry title – Jesus was called "Teacher" (44X) or "Rabbi" (19X).[254] Jesus said, "But you, do not be called 'Rabbi'; for One is your Teacher, the Christ" and "you call Me Teacher and Lord, and you say well, for so I am. If I then, your Lord and Teacher, have washed your feet, you also ought to wash one another's feet."[255]

Some elders may have the ministry gift of "teacher,"[256] but all elders must be "able to teach." Paul will say later in 1 Timothy to "let the elders who rule well be counted worthy of

---

[251] *A Commentary on the Pastoral Epistles*, Kelly, page 76.

[252] Recall that Paul wrote in Titus 1:9, "...holding fast the faithful word *as he has been taught.*"

[253] *First Timothy*, Hiebert, pages 65-66.

[254] See John 1:38, "Rabbi (which is to say, when translated, Teacher)," John 20:16, "Rabboni! (which is to say, Teacher)," and John 3:2, "Rabbi, we know that You are a teacher come from God."

[255] See Matthew 23:8 and John 13:13-14.

[256] See Ephesians 4:11; 1 Corinthians 12:28-29; Acts 13:1.

double honor, especially those whose work is preaching and *teaching*" (5:17). In order to "rule well" or to "govern well," the church leader must be able to teach well. I noticed that many commentators said something to the effect that "the church has been at its weakest when this basic requirement has been absent in its leaders" or "the failure of church leaders to know and teach the Bible is one of the chief reasons why biblical error floods our churches and drowns out the power and life of the church."[257]

Strauch's comments on this requirement of teaching sum up well what I'm trying to say in this chapter: "Like Israel, the Christian community is built on Holy Scripture, and those who oversee the community must be able to guide and protect its members by instruction from Scripture. Therefore, all elders must be 'able to teach,' which entails three basic elements: a knowledge of Scripture, the readiness to teach, and the capability to communicate. If a man cannot instruct people in the Word or protect the church from false doctrine, he does not qualify to be an elder."[258]

This ability to teach is the main difference between an elder and a deacon. A deacon by definition is someone who serves. An elder is a person who serves, but he also must teach God's people, God's word.

Using Strauch's "three basic elements" above, let's offer some practical instruction on the church leader's ability to teach.

The church leader must have a thorough knowledge of Scripture. There is no substitute for reading directly from the Word of God every day. Read, study, meditate, and do. I love that statement about Ezra the scribe in Ezra 7:10 – "For Ezra had devoted himself (was determined) to the study and observance of the Law of the Lord, and to teaching its decrees and laws in Israel." This is the heart of the elder – he wants to study so he can do; he wants to study so he can teach.

Reading through the Bible every year is an excellent way to obtain a comprehensive understanding of the Scriptures. I believe it is also important to know well key books of the Bible (obviously, all the Word is important). The gospels, Romans,

---

[257] See Guthrie, page 92; Barclay, page 92; Strauch, page 198.
[258] *Biblical Eldership*, Strauch, pages 197-198.

Proverbs, Genesis, Exodus, Isaiah, Galatians, and Revelation are key books that the elder must be thoroughly acquainted with.

If you are able to go to a school of ministry, Bible college, or seminary, please go. Learn as much as you can from the Scriptures. You will spend the rest of your life teaching from the Bible, so you should slowly obtain a comprehensive and systematic understanding of it. Obviously, this will take many years of study, so take your time and learn it carefully and in detail.

Know well the critical and essential doctrines of the Christian faith. There are many good books and resources available that cover the deity of Christ, the cross and resurrection of Christ, the Trinity, the Holy Spirit, salvation by grace, righteousness by faith, eternal judgment, God's creation, the law of God, and the true gospel, just to name a few.

I think it is important for elders to have good commentaries and studies in their library or on their computers. You will refer to them often and they will be very useful to your preparation as you develop messages and teach. Also, if you can learn Greek and Hebrew well, that will give you a tremendous advantage in your teaching. If this is not possible for you because of limited educational opportunities or time, having some good dictionaries and Bible studies explaining the original texts would be important.

The church leader must have a readiness to teach. The church elder will be teaching all the time. It might be through counseling, a home fellowship group, prayer meetings, or a time of fellowship with his friends. Many, many opportunities will be available to teach others beyond the teaching you will do from the pulpit. Be intentional. Be deliberate. "Be ready in season and out of season" to teach people God's word.

I'm assuming that most local churches will have a few elders who can teach the Bible on Sundays or during midweek services. You may lead a regular cell group or home fellowship where you have the opportunity to share from the Scriptures. I believe it is important to always have a message ready to deliver to God's people. There will be things that God will be doing in your heart month after month that need to be shared with the entire congregation. Perhaps a national or international event has happened that needs a Christian/biblical perspective. Maybe someone has died in the local church and a word of encouragement, hope, and comfort must be shared. Someone may have asked you a question that others need to hear the answer to. 1 Peter 3:15 says, "Always be prepared to give an answer to everyone who asks you to give the reason for the hope that you have."

The church leader must have the ability to communicate the Bible effectively. This is one of the most difficult skills to develop. Many elders don't know how to hold people's interest nor do they communicate God's truth well.

I love this word from Jesus in John 12:49-50: "For I did not speak of My own accord, but the Father who sent Me commanded Me what to say and how to say it...So whatever I say is just what the Father has told Me to say." *Many of us know WHAT to say, but not HOW to say it.* This is critical.

I heard someone say once, "With any presentation of truth, there must be a lot of prayer." Pray that the Holy Spirit will anoint your words and your teaching. Pray that people's minds will not wander but stay focused. Pray over all the chairs in the sanctuary or room where people will be sitting. Pray that the Lord will give you just the right examples and illustrations so that others can understand what you are saying. Good stories really help people understand what you're trying to teach. I nearly always start my sermons with an interesting story to get the attention of my audience. I've learned this about my messages: Many years later, Christians will forget the exact content of my sermon, but they will remember the stories. Personal stories or biblical examples can make your teaching come alive and help others understand.

I believe that using humor is an excellent way to spice up your message and it keeps people alert. They are definitely listening to you when you have them laughing. I use humor a lot when I'm teaching the truth. But let me caution you: Too much humor is too much. You are not a comedian full of jokes; you are a servant of God full of truth. Keep your jokes clean and let them contribute to the overall understanding of your message.

I found that the best way to teach is to teach something that is burning in your heart. If it is alive in you, you will communicate the message with fire. If you're not excited about the message, what makes you think that others will be? It's important to bring fresh bread and fresh water to feed God's people. If you are going to "feed My sheep," the grass must be wet, lush, and green. No one ever enjoys stale food.

In the next chapter, let us see two key aspects of teaching God's Word with skill. Paul wrote in Titus 2:1, "You must teach what is in accord with sound doctrine" and the elder must "encourage others by sound doctrine and refute those who oppose it" (Titus 1:9). Let's talk about encouraging and teaching others with good doctrine.

26

The Church Leader Must Encourage and Refute with Sound Doctrine

*"Holding fast the faithful word as he has been taught, **that he may be able to encourage others by sound doctrine and refute those who oppose it.**"*
(Titus 1:9)

Jesus made a well-known statement in the Synoptic gospels about who He came to help: "Those who are *well* (healthy) have no need of a physician, but those who are sick."[259] When Jesus healed the centurion's servant who was paralyzed, the Bible tells us that they "found the servant *well* who had been sick." The Lord told the man with the withered hand to "stretch out your hand," and when he did, "it was restored *whole* as the other." Great multitudes marveled at Jesus' healing power "when they saw the mute speaking, the crippled made *well*, the lame walking, and the blind seeing." When the woman with the issue of blood for twelve years was supernaturally healed, Jesus told her, "Daughter, your faith has made you well. Go in peace, and *be healed* of your affliction." Jesus asked the man at the pool of Bethesda who had an infirmity for thirty-eight years,

---

[259] Matthew 9:12; Mark 2:17; Luke 5:31.

"Do you want to be made *well*?" "Jesus said to him, 'Rise, take up your bed and walk.' And immediately the man was made *well*, took up his bed, and walked." Afterwards, when the Lord found him in the temple, He told him, "See, you have been made *well*. Sin no more, lest a worse thing come upon you." Later, when speaking of this amazing miracle, Jesus asked some Jews, "Are you angry with Me because I made a man *completely well* on the Sabbath?"[260]

All the italicized words translated "well," "whole," "healed," "healthy," or "completely well" in the above paragraph use the Greek verb (hugiainō) or adjective (hugiēs). They are words that mean "to be healthy" or "to be physically well."

This is the same Greek word that Paul uses nine times in the Pastoral Epistles for "sound" – "*sound* doctrine," "*wholesome* words," "*sound* words," "*sound* doctrine," "*sound* doctrine," "*sound* in faith," "*sound* doctrine," "*sound* in faith," and "*sound* speech."[261] *I've learned that "sound doctrine" makes Christians healthy; false doctrine makes them sick!* It is what Barclay accurately translates as "health-giving teaching" that Towner says "produces healthy believers."[262] The elder must teach God's people "sound doctrine."

Titus 1:9 defines clearly the main ministry of the elder in the local church. One translation renders it, "He must have a strong belief in the trustworthy message he was taught; then he will be able to encourage others with wholesome teaching and show those who oppose it where they are wrong," and another, "An elder must be faithful to the same true message we teach. Then he will be able to encourage others with teaching that is true and right. And he will be able to show those who are against this teaching that they are wrong." Thus, "It is clear from this that presbyter-bishops are called essentially to a teaching ministry"

---

[260] Luke 7:10; Matthew 12:13, 15:31; Mark 5:34; John 5:6-15 and 7:23.
[261] 1 Timothy 1:10, 6:3; 2 Timothy 1:13, 4:3; Titus 1:9, 1:13, 2:1, 2:2, and 2:8. Interestingly, nowhere else in Paul's letters will he use these Greek words.
[262] *The Letters to Timothy, Titus, and Philemon*, Barclay, page 267; *1-2 Timothy & Titus*, Towner, page 228. Mounce calls it "a medical metaphor," see page 392.

and "leadership in the apostolic church was largely based on proper teaching."[263]

Titus 1:9 states three important truths about elders:

First, the elder must be thoroughly trained and taught. This will take a lot of time. He "himself must keep on holding on to" the truths that he has been taught as the Greek present tense, middle voice, participle indicates (antechomenon). This verb means "to hold firmly to; cleave to." One commentator defines it as "fierce attachment."[264] In this context, it signifies that he will face opposition. One Greek dictionary defines it as "to withstand; to hold out against." Calvin writes, "Their grip on God's Word must be so strong that it must never be taken from them. A pastor should not only be learned but zealous for pure doctrine, from which he will never depart."[265] The end of Titus 1:9 shows that he will have to correct those "who oppose" sound doctrine. The elder must be a person of firm convictions and one not easily swayed by ungodly pressure or popular opinion. "A firm grasp of the truth is the indispensable preparation for him who would undertake to dispel error."[266]

Next, the elder must exhort and encourage others "by sound doctrine," literally, "in the teaching." The various Greek forms for "teaching" appear twenty-seven times in the Pastoral Letters with the noun form translated as "doctrine" sixteen times. "Exhort" is a word that indicates something "urgent." He is giving "earnest advice" that is "solemn and serious." Paul tells Titus in the next chapter, "*Exhort* the young men to be sober-minded" (2:6) and "speak these things, *exhort*, and rebuke with all authority. Let no one despise you" (2:15). Paul told Timothy, "Preach the word! Be ready in season and out of season. Convince, rebuke, *exhort*, with all longsuffering and teaching."[267] These verses reveal that both Titus and Timothy were having to say difficult and hard things to Christian believers. As needed, elders must be bold and courageous.

---

[263] *The Message of 1 Timothy & Titus*, Stott, page 178.
[264] *The Letters to Timothy and Titus*, Yarbrough, page 488.
[265] *1 & 2 Timothy & Titus*, Calvin, page 184.
[266] *Titus and Philemon*, Hiebert quoting Bernard, pages 36-37.
[267] See 2 Timothy 4:2.

Having said that, we must always remember that our doctrine should "edify," "encourage," and "build up" the body of believers. The word, "encourage," is a French word that means literally, "to cause courage." "There is always something wrong with preaching or teaching whose effect is to discourage others. The function of true Christian preachers and teachers is not to drive people to despair but to lift them up to hope."[268]

Third, the elder must "refute those who oppose" sound doctrine. Why? The next verse says because "there are many rebellious people" who are "idle talkers and deceivers." Paul goes as far as saying in verse 11, "They must be silenced, because they are ruining whole households by teaching things they ought not to teach – and that for the sake of dishonest gain." The false teachers must be silenced not the elders! The elders must speak up because these ungodly people are "ruining" (NIV), "destroying" (ERV), or "turning whole families away from the truth by their false teaching" (NLT). This is serious indeed!

Let's not forget what the Pastoral Epistles are about – Paul left Timothy and Titus in places that had false teachers teaching false doctrines. In chapter after chapter, Paul brings up the false teachings that must be dismissed and replaced with the truth. "His work as bishop relates both to the members of the flock and to the enemies of the flock. The shepherd must be able to tend the sheep and to drive away wolves."[269] Here are just a few examples:

- "Remain in Ephesus that you may charge some that they teach no other doctrine, nor give heed to fables and endless genealogies, which cause disputes rather than godly edification which is in faith."
- "Which some, having strayed, have turned aside to idle talk, desiring to be teachers of the law, understanding neither what they say nor the things which they affirm."
- "If anyone teaches otherwise and does not consent to wholesome words, even the words of our Lord Jesus Christ, and to the doctrine which accords with godliness, he is proud, knowing nothing, but is obsessed with disputes and arguments over words."

---

[268] *The Letters of Timothy, Titus, and Philemon*, Barclay, page 269.
[269] Ibid., quoting White, page 36.

- "This you know, that all those in Asia have turned away from me, among whom are Phygellus and Hermogenes."
- "Their teaching will spread like gangrene. Among them are Hymenaeus and Philetus, who have wandered away from the truth. They say that the resurrection has already taken place, and they destroy the faith of some."
- "The time will come when they will not endure sound doctrine, but according to their own desires, because they have itching ears, they will heap up for themselves teachers; and they will turn their ears away from the truth, and be turned aside to fables."
- "Cretans are always liars, evil beasts, lazy gluttons. This testimony is true. Therefore, rebuke them sharply, that they may be sound in the faith, not giving heed to Jewish fables and commandments of men who turn from the truth."[270]

So, the elder must both "encourage" and "refute." "A pastor needs two voices, one for gathering the sheep and the other for driving away wolves and thieves."[271]

I have taught and written extensively on dealing with false ministers, false doctrines, and heresies. This is a very important subject. I refer you to the footnote below for these resources.[272]

---

[270] See 1 Timothy 1:3-4, 1:6-7, 6:3-4; 2 Timothy 1:15, 2:17-18, 4:3-4; Titus 1:12-14.

[271] *1 & 2 Timothy & Titus*, Calvin, page 184.

[272] See *The False Teaching Seminar* at www.teacherofthebible.com or my books, *Detecting and Dealing with False Teaching* and my devotional commentaries *The Book of 2 Peter* and *The Book of Jude*. These two books deal more with false teachings/ministers than any other book of the Bible.

Chapter 1 – Blameless

- What is your definition of the word, "blameless?" What does this mean on a practical level?
- Why would Paul mention "blameless" or "above reproach" three times and before all other qualifications?
- What is your perspective on the man in pages 4-5 who wanted a leadership position in the author's church?

Chapter 2 – A Good Reputation

- In your own words, why does the devil get into a church if we appoint unqualified leaders? (See page 13)
- Why do you think that the real test of a person's character is from Monday to Saturday, not Sunday morning? (See page 15)
- Read Psalm 15:4. Why does keeping your promise (word) hurt? Why does it cost us? (See page 16)

Chapter 3 – Of Good Behavior

- What impressed you the most about David Riester? Why? (See pages 19-20)
- Read Daniel 6:1-5. In your own words, why did Daniel have such a blameless character?
- How would you define the word, "kosimos?" (See page 20)

Chapter 4 – A Lover of Good Things

- What point was the author trying to make when he wrote, "If you look for dirt, you'll be sure to find it?" (See page 28)
- List three good things you see in your current pastor?
- Why are "orphans" and "widows" so important to Father God? (James 1:27)

Chapter 5 – Hospitable

- Do you reach out to new people and visitors at your church? Why or why not?
- Read Matthew 25:35-46. What does it mean practically to "take in strangers?"
- What are some things that your local church can do to be more hospitable to members and visitors?

Chapter 6 – Temperate

- In your own words, define "temperate" and explain why it is so important in the life of an elder.
- In your own words, what happened to Moses in Psalm 106:32-33?
- What is the best way to calm someone down when they are angry? Explain.

Chapter 7 – Sober-Minded

- Which statistic about alcohol stood out for you and why? (See pages 41-42)
- Spiritually speaking, what does it mean to be sober?
- What is wrong with the belief that if a pastor has a big church that means he's a great minister? (See page 45)

Chapter 8 – Self-Controlled

- Why did James and John want to call fire down on the Samaritans (Luke 9:54-56)? What was wrong with them?
- What point was the author trying to make when he wrote, "We will quickly burnout doing what God told everyone else to do?" (See pages 50-51)
- "If you're bit by a snake, don't become one." Comment. (See page 50)

Chapter 9 – Just

- What went through your mind when you read about Ricky Jackson's injustice? (See pages 55-56)
- In your own words, what does it mean that the Lord is a "just God?" (See Psalm 7:11 and Revelation 15:3)
- Martin Luther King Jr. said, "Injustice anywhere is a threat to justice everywhere." Why is this true?

Chapter 10 – Holy

- Is it possible for a Christian "to be holy as the Lord is holy?" Explain.
- Jerry Bridges wrote, "As we grow in holiness, we grow in hatred of sin." Why is this true? (See page 61)
- What practical steps can an elder do to keep himself sexually pure? (See pages 61-62).

Chapter 11 – Gentle

- What can men and elders do to cultivate the spirit of gentleness in their lives?
- When facing tense situations, why must elders always approach people with gentleness?
- Does gentleness mean weakness? Explain.

Chapter 12 – Not Quarrelsome

- Think of someone you know who is angry and quarrelsome. Why is this person this way?
- What happened between Paul and Barnabas in Acts 15:36-40? What was the root problem?
- What will begin to happen in a local church if one of the elders is quarrelsome?

Chapter 13 – Not Violent

- According to Jude 23, why do we have to be cautious when we minister to those coming out of evil lifestyles?
- What was wrong with the author's reaction to the man who turned to drugs? (See pages 78-80)
- Do you think what Nehemiah did in Nehemiah 13:25 was acceptable in God's sight? Why or why not?

Chapter 14 – Not Soon Angry

- How should elders react toward people who leave the church?
- The author quotes James 1:20 and says that "anger never works." Is this true? Why or why not?
- What is happening spiritually in a local church when the leaders begin speaking evil of one another?

Chapter 15 – Not Self-Willed

- How a person responds to correction says a lot about him/her? Why is this true?
- Abraham Lincoln once said, "If you want to test a man's character, give him power." Why is this true?
- Peter told elders in 1 Peter 5:3 not to "lord it over people." What does that mean?

Chapter 16 – Not Greedy for Money

- Is it really true that most ministers are greedy for money? Or do a few greedy preachers taint all the others?
- What are your thoughts about the elderly lady who gave the author $200 per week for six weeks?
- The author says that an elder greedy for money is a cancer to the soul of the church. Why so?

Chapter 17 – Not Covetous

- Why is greed or covetousness such a "deadly" sin in the church?
- As you consider Balaam's life (Jude 11; 2 Peter 2:15; Numbers 22), what reveals his covetousness?
- Why is contentment with God an antidote to the love of money or covetousness?

Chapter 18 – Not Given to Wine

- What are your beliefs about drinking alcohol, beer, wine, or liquor among Christians?
- Read Romans 14. If a Christian doesn't want to drink, does that make him legalistic? Why or why not?
- If you went to your pastor's house and you saw him drinking a beer, how would that effect your view of him?

Chapter 19 – Not a Novice

- Why will the devil get into a local church that appoints a novice as an elder?
- Calvin says that new Christians are often bold, impetuous, and full of self-confidence? Why is this bad?
- What's the advantage of appointing an older man who has lived a godly life versus someone who is very young?

Chapter 20 – Husband of One Wife

- Explain what "one wife husband" means.
- Do you believe that a person who has been divorced is disqualified from being an elder? Why or why not?
- What are three things every Christian can do to strengthen his marriage?

Chapter 21 – Rules His Household Well

- In your own words, why does looking carefully at a potential elder's children a good indicator of how he will "rule" in the church?
- Do you agree that a potential candidate for eldership must be a good dad before he will ever be a good elder? Why?
- Read Alexander Strauch's comments on pages 129-130. What stands out for you in what he wrote?

Chapter 22 – Believing Children

- Should a potential elder be disqualified if one of his children is not a believer? Explain.
- Do you agree with the author's comments on education and schooling on pages 134-135? Why or why not?
- 1 Corinthians 15:33 says, "Evil company corrupts good habits." Should our children play with unbelievers?

Chapter 23 – Obedient Children

- Describe the behavior of a submissive child.
- What does the author mean when he writes that obedience and submission only work "from the bottom up?"
- How can a father model a humble, submissive attitude toward his wife and children? What must he do?

Chapter 24 – Not Wild Children

- Should the pastor whose fourteen-year-old daughter got pregnant have resigned? Why or why not?
- Why do you think the prophet Samuel's children ended up becoming so rebellious?
- Do you think it is necessary to discipline our young children with a paddle (rod) like Proverbs says? Why?

Chapter 25 – Able to Teach

- Why do so many pastors and churches only look at a man's abilities and not his character and family?
- What are some of the key aspects of an elder who teaches the Bible well? What makes an effective communicator?
- The author says that "the best way to teach is to teach something that is burning in your heart." What does he mean by that?

Chapter 26 – Encourage and Refute

- What does the author mean by the statement that "sound doctrine makes Christians healthy; false doctrine makes them sick?" Why is good doctrine so important to church health?
- Paul wrote in 2 Timothy 4:3-4 that a time was coming when Christians would not endure "sound doctrine" but gather false teachers who would "turn their ears away from the truth." Name some teachings that are turning believers away from the truth?
- What does the author mean when he writes, "To rule well or to govern well, the church leader must be able to teach well?" How does ruling correlate to teaching? (See page 155)

THE BIBLICAL QUALIFICATIONS OF CHURCH LEADERS

About the Author

Charlie Avila is the Senior Pastor of Clovis Christian Center in Fresno, California. He is married to Irma and has two adult children – Leah (husband: Jose) and Daniel. Pastor Charlie is the Bible teacher of the Spirit of Wisdom and Revelation teaching newsletters and the principal teacher on the Teacher of the Bible website.

He is an instructor with the Fresno School of Mission and other ministry schools. He has spoken in conferences and churches locally, nationally, and internationally. He teaches special seminars on various Bible subjects and verse by verse studies through Old Testament and New Testament books. He has written several books available on Amazon including *The Christian and Anger*, *The Christian and Homosexuality*, *The Christian and Hell*, *The Christian & Witchcraft*, *Detecting & Dealing with False Teachings*, *Healing the Sick*, *How to Become a Christian*, *The End Times*, *Making Disciples One on One*, *Having Sex with Your Boyfriend*, *Witnessing to Jehovah's Witnesses*, *The Biblical Qualifications of Church Leaders*, *Premarital Counseling for Christian Couples* and various commentaries on books of the Bible including Esther, 2 Peter, and Jude. He also has many books in Spanish by the same titles as the English versions.

He can be contacted at teacherofthebible@gmail.com or Clovis Christian Center, 3606 N. Fowler Ave, Fresno, CA 93727-1124.

Selected Bibliography
(By Author)

This list is ordered by the author's last name. We quoted from thirteen other commentaries and books, but chose only to list those books that cover 1 Timothy 3 and Titus 1. See footnotes for other references.

The Letters to Timothy, Titus, and Philemon, William Barclay, The New Daily Study Bible, Westminster John Knox Press, 2003, 321 pages.
- I probably quoted from Barclay more than any other commentator. Very good background material on Titus and Timothy's situations and the meanings of various Greek words. Offers his own translation of the Greek text which often provided insightful understanding. Highly recommended.

1 & 2 Timothy & Titus, John Calvin, The Crossway Classic Commentaries, Crossway Books, 1998, 208 pages.
- Overall, a good commentary with much quotable material. Some of his comments were very brief. For example, his entire commentary on Titus 1:5-9 was only five pages. Gave good instruction on the elder's teaching ministry.

1 and 2 Timothy, Titus, Gordon D. Fee, New International Biblical Commentary, Hendrickson Publishers, 1988, 332 pages.
- Although a first-rate scholar who has written some incredible commentaries and studies over the decades, this commentary was often dull and uninspiring.

Ancient Christian Commentary on Scripture, Colossians, 1-2 Thessalonians, 1-2 Timothy, Titus, Philemon, Edited by Peter Gorday, Volume IX, Inter-Varsity Press, 2000, 346 pages.
- While there were some occasional good comments on the elder's qualifications, this "ancient" commentary suffered from the fact that there were not a lot of comments by the

early church fathers on 1 Timothy 3:1-7 and Titus 1:5-9. Most of the comments were from Jerome or Chrysostom.

The Pastoral Epistles, Donald Guthrie, Tyndale New Testament Commentaries, Revised Edition, Inter-Varsity Press, 1996, 240 pages.

- Very good commentary. He was especially good in dealing with the elder's home life including relationships with his wife and children. Also, it was good on relationships with outsiders. I quoted him often and I like how he gets to the point quickly.

First Timothy, D. Edmond Hiebert, Everyman's Bible Commentary, Moody Press, 1957, 127 pages.

- As we have come to expect for Dr. Hiebert, his commentary was fair, sane, and level-headed. Interacts well with other commentaries available back in his day. Offered good comments on the qualifications of sober-minded, reputation with outsiders, and the elder's children.

Titus and Philemon, D. Edmond Hiebert, Everyman's Bible Commentary, Moody Press, 1957, 128 pages.

- Very similar to his commentary on 1 Timothy. Very good comments on the elder's teaching ministry and the qualifications of "self-controlled" and "no striker."

A Commentary on the Pastoral Epistles, J. N. D. Kelly, Thornapple Commentaries, Baker Book House, 1963, 264 pages.

- Like Hiebert, another no-nonsense commentary. Offers his own translation, which often used very archaic wording. Gave good historical background on the situation dealt with by Timothy and Titus in their respective cities and congregations.

The Pastoral Epistles, George W. Knight III, The New International Greek Testament Commentary (NIGTC), Eerdmans Publishing Company, 1992, 514 pages.

- Long recognized as one of the best and most comprehensive studies on the Pastoral Epistles, Knight's commentary was good. His definitions of the qualifications for elders were especially good.

Pastoral Epistles, William D. Mounce, Word Biblical Commentary, Zondervan Publishing, 2000, 641 pages.
- Certainly the longest commentary on the Pastoral Epistles. Mounce leaves no stone unturned. He covers comprehensively all the available data and studies on these letters. I found that what he was saying was already said by someone else. Not a lot of original exegesis. Overall, however, it was a good commentary.

The Message of 1 Timothy & Titus: Guard the Truth, John R. W. Stott, The Bible Speaks Today, Inter-Varsity Press, 1996, 232 pages.
- As with all of Stott's books, he gives excellent reasons for his conclusions and has a great way of expressing difficult truths in simple language. He gave very good definitions on many of the qualifications. Highly recommended.

Biblical Eldership: An Urgent Call to Restore Biblical Church Leadership, Alexander Strauch, Second Edition, Lewis and Roth Publishers, 1988, 288 pages.
- One of the best books ever written on church eldership. I strongly recommend all church leaders read this book. Straightforward, no-nonsense, and drawing powerful conclusions, this book reveals an author who cares deeply about the local church leadership of today. Not only does it cover Titus 1 and 1 Timothy 3 thoroughly, it also teaches from all the main New Testament texts on elders. Strauch advocates strongly for male-only elders.

1-2 Timothy & Titus, Philip H. Towner, The IVP New Testament Commentary Series, Inter-Varsity Press, 1994, 271 pages.
- I had never read any of Towner's commentaries before and I was surprised with how insightful he was on so many points. He gives excellent background information

on many of the qualifications especially on "hospitality" and the elder's marriage.

The Letters of Timothy and Titus, Robert W. Yarbrough, The Pillar New Testament Commentary, Eerdmans Publishing Company, 2018, 603 pages.

- This is one of the best commentaries on the Pastoral Epistles, if not the best. Very comprehensive. His background study to 1 Timothy 3:1-7 was excellent especially his explanation of "must" (dei) and how it is used in these three letters. The leaders *must* have these qualifications. Highly recommended.

Scriptural Reference Index

Made in the USA
Columbia, SC
26 November 2024

47165574R10108